Everett Leadingham, Editor

Though this book is designed for group study, it is also intended for personal enjoyment and spiritual growth. A leader's guide is available from your local bookstore or your publisher.

Beacon Hill Press of Kansas City
Kansas City, Missouri

Copyright 2005
By Beacon Hill Press of Kansas City
Kansas City, Missouri

ISBN: 083-412-1611

Printed in the United States of America

Editor: Everett Leadingham
Managing Editor: Charlie L. Yourdon
Executive Editor: Merritt J. Nielson

Cover Design: Paul Franitza

10 9 8 7 6 5 4 3 2 1

Contents

Why, O LORD, *do you stand far off?*
Why do you hide yourself in times of trouble?

Psalm 10:1

Where can I go from your Spirit?
Where can I flee from your presence?
If I go up to the heavens,
you are there;
if I make my bed in the depths,
you are there.

Psalm 139:7-8

CHAPTER 1

When the World Is Violent

by Rebecca Laird

DURING ADVENT one year, the Scriptures we read on Sunday seemed incongruous to the nightly news. In church we read, "For to us a child is born . . . And he will be called Wonderful Counselor, Mighty God, Everlasting Father, Prince of Peace. Of the increase of his government and peace there will be no end" (Isaiah 9:6-7).

Within a week, a man consumed by racial rage shot and killed six commuters returning from New York City. I live close to where this tragedy occurred and regularly travel to the city by train. I could have easily been one of his victims. Where was the Prince of Peace and His peaceful government? It seemed rather that "of *violence* there will be no end."

The next week, my family traveled to Denver to visit relatives. The day we arrived, a disgruntled, ex-employee at a pizza parlor murdered his former boss. A few days later, the media reported a threat from a disturbed soul who vowed to shoot Santa in a mall. The area shopping centers closed every "Santa Land." We parents tried to answer our bewildered children's question, "Why does somebody want to kill Santa Claus?"

On Sunday we sang, "Hark! the herald angels sing '. . . Peace on earth, and mercy mild—God and sinners reconciled.'" Where was that reconciliation?

With all this lawlessness and violence not far from my

mind, my family joined the worldwide Christian church in retelling the glorious story: "Suddenly a great company of the heavenly host appeared with the angel, praising God and saying, 'Glory to God in the highest, and on earth peace to men on whom his favor rests'" (Luke 2:13-14).

In a stable, God humbly entered into the human struggle as a helpless Baby. The Child grew and took upon His shoulders the sins (violence and brokenness) of His brothers and sisters of the world. As an adult, Jesus called many to join Him in living a new way.

That Christmas, I wondered anew about the teachings of Jesus. Especially His proclamation, "Blessed are the peacemakers, for they will be called [children] of God" (Matthew 5:9). Peacemakers are few and far between. Violence rages. What does it mean for us to be people of peace in a society where those who love guns and hate others (and probably themselves) hold us hostage to fear?

The Problem of Violence

Violence isn't a new phenomenon. Assuming that ancient times were more peaceful is wishful thinking. Jesus was born into Palestine where Roman rule was heavy and oppression was real. Cross the Romans and end up on a cross. Thousands were crucified for rebelling. Almost everybody was hoping for a messiah to come and end the political tyranny. Then, Jesus arrived—teaching nonviolence, noncooperation with evil, and love for our enemies!

Jesus did not appear as a conquering, political king. He came as a Suffering Servant who called those who would follow to love enemies—even oppressors!—with a deep love that supersedes unjust treatment. Jesus commanded that we respond with love, even risk receiving further damage, rather than take revenge or repay the offender like we have been wrongly treated.

Why did Jesus do this? Because to Jesus, those who kill and maim are not enemies deserving retaliation. They are in need of forgiveness. As He said on the way to the Cross, "Father, forgive them, for they do not know what they are doing" (Luke 23:34).

Immediately after Jesus told us that peacemakers are blessed, He went on to preach in the Sermon on the Mount: "You have heard that it was said, 'Eye for eye, and tooth for tooth.' But I tell you, Do not resist an evil person. If someone strikes you on the right cheek, turn to him the other also" (Matthew 5:38-39).

I hear this verse and think, *Perhaps I would let someone strike me for the sake of love.* Yet today, fighting isn't done with hands; it's done with pistols, semiautomatic weapons, missiles, and nuclear warheads. If we let someone shoot once, there will be no need to turn the other cheek. We'll already be dead.

So what about Jesus' teaching? What does Matthew 5:38-39 mean? Ron Sider, in *Christ and Violence,* offers two insights. First, it means that "one should not resist evil persons by exacting equal damages for injury suffered." Second, it means that "one should not respond to an evil person by placing him in the category of enemy. Indeed, one should love one's enemies, even at great personal cost. The good of the other person, not one's own needs or rights are decisive."[1]

Let me illustrate. A tormented, young man in our community shot and killed a wonderful church woman. She was a saint and certainly didn't deserve it. She deserved a long life and lots of love. He, too, had gone to church, but sporadically. By murdering this woman, he became an enemy, someone to be feared and avoided.

What was the church to do? Buy guns and patrol the community to protect the single women? Never reach out to another tormented young man? And what about the murderer, a person for whom Christ died? We must—but who will?—continue to pray, visit, and love the unlovable. What hard words these are to live!

Does this mean that we must take every wrong done to us without a word? Or sit idly by as kids carry guns and kill each other for fun or out of frustration?

No. No. Absolutely, no!

Jesus compels us to be peacemakers, but not to lie down in the face of evil. We are to be clear and active in our noncooperation with evil. Jesus lived and ultimately died amid violence, all the while proclaiming and embodying the values of the kingdom of God. Jesus taught and lived forgiveness, holy power, and sacrificial love.

We are also required to be involved in peacemaking in our own cities and towns. We can't proclaim peace from the pulpits and pews without doing what we can to preserve the sacredness of human life in our homes, on our streets, and in our neighborhoods.

When we consider the mortal violence all around us, Jesus' call to respond to lawlessness with tough (that is, nonsentimental) love challenges our commitments and models of ministry. We aren't called necessarily to wrestle guns out of the hands of thugs. Jesus isn't asking for martyrs, but for followers who will act truthfully and let the outcome be left in God's hands—even at the risk of martyrdom. Remember, survival and safety are not gospel promises. Look at Jesus and His disciples: only a few lived to a ripe, old age.

Lethal violence demands a savvy response. When one person kills another, the one with the gun treats the other person as a thing. Christians cannot do that. People—all people—are created in the image of God. We can't shoot back; but we can fight back with love, courage, and shrewdness while balancing the issues of justice and mercy.

Violence and Values

How then do we deter violence? The key to reducing violence is found in imparting Kingdom values. What makes people kill and maim others?

Recently, a reporter for *TIME* magazine asked some teenagers in a Midwestern city why they bought, carried, and used guns. One said, "It was always really violent around my house." One reason people resort to violence is they see others act in violent ways. Violence breeds violence. When kids watch parents, older siblings, and television heroes use force to get what they want, they copy what they see.

The magazine reporter also said that kids used guns as "a defense against the inexplicable despair that torments so many . . . teenagers." Despair is living without hope. Many kids today spend their tender years with absent or too-busy parents. The voices that many hear for hours each day are those of older kids in the neighborhood who have discovered that guns bring a sense of power. In overly simplistic terms, some embrace the values of violence that say, "So what if we never have a stable family? So what if we don't go to school and can't get a job? There aren't any jobs anyway! Nobody cares about me; why should I care about anyone or anything else? Why not get a gun and use it? I probably won't live to adulthood anyway. If people won't respect me, at least they will fear me."

Last, the reporter wrote, "Some days, guns are just a defense against boredom that comes from a lack of guidance and direction."[2] Many kids are left to their own devices, and guns are at least one form of excitement. Having a group of kids that will take their side no matter what happens is almost as good as having a loving family. Most will take belonging to a gang over going it alone. That's very human of them.

The Church as an Agent of Peace

Violence is rooted in misplaced values. People kill because they don't understand that life is a sacred gift from God. Ironic, isn't it, that one of the clearest commandments we have is, "You shall not murder" (Exodus 20:13)? How come these kids never learned this? If parents and schools failed to teach basic values, where was the Church?

People also resort to violence because they feel powerless, unloved, and outcast. Our Bible proclaims, "A father to the fatherless, a defender of widows, is God in his holy dwelling. God sets the lonely in families" (Psalm 68:5-6). Are we emulating our God? Are we mentoring the kids without parents? Are we defending and including the vulnerable in our communities?

People resort to violence because they have no hope. Certainly one of the things the Church has in quantity is hope. Hebrews 10:23-24 says, "Let us hold unswervingly to the hope we profess, for he who promised is faithful. And let us consider how we may spur one another on toward love and good deeds." What are we doing to encourage one another to declare peace and show love in the world and in our neighborhoods?

Christians are called, not to be violent but to value the sanctity of life. We preach that all are welcome in the family of God and that hope is available through faith. The Church has something vital to offer as an alternative to violence.

Just as the Christmas of violence I described above erupted, nearly 50 religious leaders from across the country praised the president of the United States for his declaration of values as central to curbing violence. The letter they sent to the White House said, "The battle against violence begins in each of our hearts and lives. Religious faith offers vital moral resources for replacing fear and violence with hope and reconciliation in our homes, communities, and nation.[3]

Here are a few examples of what various churches are doing to instill values that promote peace and deter violence.

Prevention programs: The best time to deter violence is before it begins.

A minister in central New Jersey says, "There aren't

many institutions set up to win people over to a value system. It's up to the church to show that a prescribed set of values is possible."[4] One of the concrete things his church does is to have all of the children bring in their report cards, which are entered into a data base. Any child that gets under a "B" is given a tutor. Additionally, boys from single-parent families are paired with men as role models.

A church in San Francisco opened its doors and invited the addicts in the neighborhood to come in and talk about why they smoked crack cocaine. Drug addiction and violence go hand in glove. Many crimes are committed to obtain money for drugs, and many violent acts are committed by persons under the influence of drugs and alcohol. The addicts talked about smoking crack to deaden the pain of family abuse, shame, and deprivation. As relationships began and the church became an extended family for the addicts, a grassroots recovery program was designed by the recovering addicts and spread out into the community. Violent crime decreased in their neighborhood.

Another church in California hosted a course for parents of children at risk in the local elementary school. Parents were recruited through personal calls and mailings by the program director. The church provided the facility, baby-sitters, tutors, and follow-up. Parishioners came and cheered on the graduates who completed the 12-week course on positive parenting skills.

Outreach programs: Many persons don't belong to a local congregation. Thus, the church must stay in or go to troubled neighborhoods and offer hope and help.

Groups of people from various churches rallied in Maryland to support handgun legislation and stood vigil on corners frequented by drug dealers. Nothing is so successful in deterring drugs and crime as good people banding together with their eyes wide open.

In Oakland, California, a congregation in an inner-city neighborhood facilitated dialogue sessions between gang members and local police. Church members, along with representatives from other denominations, held weekly prayer vigils at the site of the numerous homicides committed earlier in the year. The church also responded to a request to help stop vandalism by sponsoring block parties in the neighborhoods where vandalism and violence reigned. People got to know each other and began working together. Vandalism fell drastically.

It is well-known that crime soars in the summer months when kids are bored and unsupervised. In the northeast, a group of college students designed a program for the teens in a high-crime housing project during after-school and summer hours. The students staffed a community center that offered an alternative to violence. Many kids chose basketball games and trips to the beach over driving around town aimlessly with loaded guns ready to use on a whim. As one youth worker in the Bronx said, "Kids aren't stupid. If you offer them a clean glass of water or a dirty glass of water, they'll take the clean one." Sadly, too few glasses of clean water are being offered.

Many churches have taken on violence by committing to prison ministries. People coming out of prison are at risk to commit further crimes, as many remain without jobs, support, or motivation to reenter society. The families of the incarcerated also are at high risk of continuing the cycle of violence and criminal behavior without the intervention of others who model a different way of living.

Political action: In San Francisco, a local church invited the precinct police to come to the church and teach the congregation how to protect themselves and deter others from violence. A community watch was organized and neighbors began to patrol their neighborhoods and assist those in need. The church gained the respect of its neighbors and several started coming to church as a result. They realized that the church cared about the community.

In New York state, clergy launched a campaign against

handguns and semiautomatic weapons and met with media executives to complain about violence in programming and reporting on news shows. To complement this program, clergy vowed to encourage boycotts of advertisers that sponsored violent programming.

In Petaluma, California, local churches rallied and petitioned lawmakers to pass a "three-strikes-you're-out" law that would mandate life sentences for repeat felons.

The church has power to teach values, advocate for good, and resist evil and violence. Promoting peace will challenge us deeply.

So, Where Is God?

With the increasing volume of violence all around us, we may be tempted to ask, "Where are You, God?" We might even ask ourselves (in a voice hopefully loud enough for God to eavesdrop), "Who's winning this battle between good and evil?" Goodness, peace, and love? Or sin, hate, and violence? The newspapers seem to report the score in favor of the latter, but the view from the newspapers doesn't cover the whole story.

As Christians, we have the assurance that while violence may appear to have the upper hand, there is more to life than can be seen. The steadily growing, relentless kingdom of God moves ahead in ways sometimes too subtle for human perception. That's the way the Kingdom has impacted our violent world from the day an innocent Baby was born in a manger while would-be assassins lurked in the shadows. God's kingdom is winning and will ultimately disarm those whose aim is destruction and violence. It is this indisputable hope that carries those who day after day offer peace and love to their troubled world.

The story is told that after the crumbling of the Iron Curtain and the abrupt end of decades of communistic rule in one of the eastern European countries, a Protestant church reopened. The church board met to decide what message should be put on their outside sign to alert the town that the church was again in operation, having survived the violent and atheistic leadership imposed on them.

After prayerful and careful consideration, the board posted this simple message, "The Lamb wins!" In spite of the power of the seemingly invincible communist state, in the end the Kingdom was declared the winner. And not just at the end; the Kingdom was winning all along.

The Lamb wins! In the face of violence, injustice, corruption, and sin, God is working His purposes out through those of us who claim the name of Christ. We know that the Prince of Peace has come, and we, as His followers, have been empowered to do all we can to bring peace to our tumultuous society. God is working in our hearts and minds and efforts to combat violence. He does not abandon us; He sustains us in the midst of the battle.

Scripture Cited: Exodus 20:13; Psalm 68:5-6; Isaiah 9:6-7; Luke 2:13-14; Matthew 5:9, 38-39; Hebrews 10:23

About the Author: Rebecca Laird is a writer and editor specializing in adult spirituality and social renewal. She is coauthor of *No Hiding Place: Recovery and Empowerment for Our Troubled Communities.*

CHAPTER 2

When War Destroys People and Property

by C. S. Cowles

IT WAS A PICTURE that seared its way into the consciousness of a whole generation. It showed a screaming, young Vietnamese girl running naked down a country road, her body enveloped in flames, her arms flung outward, her eyes wild with terror. Her village had just been hit with an aerial napalm attack. The photo won a Pulitzer prize for Associated Press photographer Nick Ut, and turned our nation from grudging support of the Vietnam War into fierce opposition.

Seldom has one picture constituted such a defining moment. The tower of justifications for that war—stopping the cancerous spread of godless Communism—came crashing down when we were forced to ask whether the cure had become worse than the curse. "Beware," warned Nietzsche, "that in fighting monsters you do not become a monster."[1]

Where was God in that devastating scene? And where is God in all the violence and carnage going on in the world today? Where was God when our son-in-law's best friend was blown to pieces by an Iraqi roadside bomb? We can identify with the psalmist who cried out in anguish, "O righteous God . . . bring to an end the violence of the wicked and make the righteous secure" (Psalm 7:9).

We will no more arrive at a satisfactory answer to these kinds of questions than Job did. Nevertheless, we can

briefly survey some of the ways in which our Scriptures
and the Church address these complex issues, and hopefully gain some insights that will enable us to find a "place
of shelter" in the midst of "the tempest and storm" of
"wars and rumors of wars" (Psalm 55:8; Matthew 24:6).

The Source of Conflict

Social biologists, such as Nobel prize recipient Konrad
Lorenz, contend that conflict is a necessary and inescapable
fact of life. Every living organism is endowed with sufficient aggressive drives to wrest from a passive and resistant
environment what it must have in order to survive. Even
the tiniest baby is equipped with well-developed lungs and
vocal chords guaranteed to shatter the equilibrium of
everyone in earshot until its compelling needs are met.
Likewise, all living organisms possess potent weapons to
defend themselves against whatever threatens their well-
being. It is at the vortex where these aggressive drives and
resistive instincts collide that the hurricanes of conflict are
generated. Violence, they say, is prevalent in life.[2]

The Scriptures, on the other hand, paint a portrait of a
violence-free creation, where in the beginning "God saw
all that he had made, and it was very good" (Genesis 1:31).
They also point ahead to a time when God will inaugurate
"a new heaven and a new earth" in which "there will be no
more death or mourning or crying or pain, for the old order of things has passed away" (Revelation 21:1, 4).

Where then did things go so terribly wrong? Paul's
answer is as succinct as it is profound. "Sin entered the
world through one man, and death through sin, and in this
way death came to all men, because all [have] sinned" (Romans 5:12). "What causes fights and quarrels among you?"
asks James. "Don't they come from your desires that battle
within you? You want something but don't get it. You kill
and covet, but you cannot have what you want. You quar-
rel and fight" (4:1-2). What an accurate, if bleak, portrait of

our fallen world's landscape! Because "all have sinned and fall short of the glory of God" and because "the wages of sin is death" (Romans 3:23; 6:23), wars and rumors of wars will continue to be an inescapable part of our human condition until Jesus comes again.

It is in light of this reality that we turn to the Scriptures. We confess, at the outset, that the signals we get are decidedly mixed.

The God of War

In his article, "Why I Use 'Fighting Words,'" James Dobson points out that "today's defenders of righteousness did not invent the analogy to warfare." He recalls growing up in the church, singing "Onward Christian soldiers! Marching as to war," "Stand up, stand up for Jesus, Ye soldiers of the cross," as well as "The Battle Hymn of the Republic." Dobson adds, "That sounds very much like the language of war to me."[3]

While Dobson makes it clear that he is speaking of warfare "against the spiritual forces of evil" (Ephesians 6:12), it is equally clear in the Old Testament that Yahweh's battles are quite physical—fire and flood, plague and pestilence, disease and death. Battles are waged with marching armies, thrusting spears, and slashing swords. They involve bloodshed. Slaughter. Mutilation. Pillage. Rape. Destruction. And genocide.

Jihad, "holy war," did not originate with Islam. It was not Mohammed but Moses who led the Israelites in a "praise and worship service" following the Exodus. The song they sang included these lyrics: "The LORD is a warrior; the LORD is his name. . . . [His] right hand . . . shattered the enemy" (Exodus 15:3, 6). The name "Israel" can mean "God [El] does battle." Yahweh as a warrior pervades every Old Testament book except Ruth, Song of Solomon, and Esther. Israel's enemies were Yahweh's enemies, and their wars were His wars. Yahweh fought for the

Israelites, and sometimes against them. Isaiah's oracle against Babylon is typical of the hundreds of passages in the Old Testament where God either acts violently or threatens violence:

> I have commanded my holy ones; I have summoned my warriors to carry out my wrath . . . The LORD Almighty is mustering an army for war. . . . to destroy the whole country. . . . See, the day of the LORD is coming—a cruel day, with wrath and fierce anger—to make the land desolate and destroy the sinners within it. . . . Whoever is captured will be thrust through; all who are caught will fall by the sword. Their infants will be dashed to pieces before their eyes; their houses will be looted and their wives ravished (Isaiah 13:3-16).

While we may be appalled at the scope, frequency, and viciousness of Yahweh's punishments, it posed no moral problem for the ancient Israelites. To the contrary, God's wrath was seen as an inevitable and necessary outcome of His three basic attributes: sovereignty, holiness, and personality. Unlike Baal, Asherah, Marduk, and other Near Eastern gods of war, Yahweh was not violent in His nature. His "burning anger" (Exodus 15:7) was stirred up by the waywardness and wickedness of people. Typical is His warning to the newly liberated Israelites that if they engage in immorality or idolatry or "mistreat an alien" or "take advantage of a widow or an orphan," then "My anger will be aroused, and I will kill you with the sword. . . . You are to be my holy people" (Exodus 22:21-22, 24, 31).

The God of Peace

The New Testament is as devoid of wars and battles as the Old Testament is full. With the coming of the "Prince of Peace" (Matthew 1:23; Isaiah 9:6), it is clear that a new day in salvation history has dawned. It is a fact of inexhaustible significance that Jesus never used His supernatural power to hurt, maim, coerce, conquer, or destroy. He was the embodiment of God's servant who "will not shout or cry out, or raise his voice in the streets. A bruised reed He will not break, and a smoldering wick he will not snuff out" (Isaiah 42:2-3).

The God disclosed in Jesus is not one who summons His "warriors to carry out [His] wrath," much less does He will the genocidal annihilation of any peoples or nations. When the angry disciples wanted to call fire down from heaven upon recalcitrant Samaritans, Jesus "turned and rebuked them. And he said, 'You do not know what kind of spirit you are of, for the Son of Man did not come to destroy men's lives, but to save them'" (Luke 9:55, footnote). Clearly, the spirit that wants to see people burn, like the nine-year-old Vietnamese girl, is not of God.

God in the New Testament is never defined as a warrior but rather "the God of peace" (Romans 15:33; Philippians 4:9; 1 Thessalonians 5:23; Hebrews 13:20) or "the Lord of Peace" (2 Thessalonians 3:16). It is not "holy warriors" who will be called "sons of God," but "peacemakers" (Matthew 5:9). Jesus not only countermanded Moses' laws of vengeance but commanded love of enemies (Matthews 5:38-48; Luke 6:27-36). A careful study of Jesus' teachings on nonviolence reveals that He does not advocate doormat pacifism but active, nonviolent resistance. Or as Paul put it, "Bless those who persecute you. . . . Do not be overcome by evil, but overcome evil with good" (Romans 12:14, 21). Although Jesus could have summoned "more than twelve legions of angels" to fight for Him (Matthew 26:53), instead He prayed a prayer never before spoken by anyone in recorded history—a prayer so astonishing, so radical, so awe-inspiring that we have yet to plumb its profound depths. "Father, forgive them, for they do not know what they are doing" (Luke 23:34).

To Peter's abortive attempt to defend his Master in Gethsemane, Jesus responded: "Put your sword back in its place . . . for all who draw the sword will die by the sword" (Matthew 26:52). Peter must have taken Jesus' rebuke to heart, for decades later he wrote, "Christ suffered for you, leaving you an example, that you should follow in his steps . . . When they hurled their insults at him, he did not retaliate; when he suffered, he made no threats. Instead, he entrusted himself to him who judges justly" (1 Peter 2:21, 23).

War and Peace in Church History

Mahatma Gandhi observed that the only people on earth who do not see Jesus and His teachings as nonviolent are Christians. Not so the earliest believers. They were so sure that the call to follow Christ was a commitment to nonviolence that for the first three centuries, they would rather die than fight, and did so by the tens of thousands. To literally "follow in [Christ's] steps" meant that their mission was not to conquer but convert, not to fight but forgive, not to destroy but heal. Yet, armed with no rhetoric other than the gospel of peace and no weapons but love, these followers of the Prince of Peace conquered Rome without drawing a sword.

All of that changed with the conversion of Emperor Constantine in the fourth century, and the edict declaring Christianity to be the official religion of the Roman Empire. When that happened, the well-being of the Church merged with that of the Empire. Augustine, the most influential theologian after Paul, was the first to formulate a doctrine of "just war." Ironically, what prompted Augustine to abandon three centuries of strict adherence to Jesus' ethic of nonviolence was his inability to bring the schismatic Donatists—the "holiness people" of his time—under the ecclesiastical umbrella of the Catholic bishop whom they regarded as corrupt. When he enlisted the services of the Roman army to force the Donatists back into the fold, he unleashed a "terrible and swift sword" that Christians have been using to kill not only pagans and infidels, but fellow Christians ever since, with our own nation's devastating Civil War being only one case in point.

John Wesley, who described himself as a "lover of peace," abhorred war, and worked ceaselessly against it. In his open letter to his fellow Englishmen on the eve of war with the American Colonies, he speaks of war as "a terrible evil," and utterly "monstrous." That "there is war in the world! War between men! War between Christians" was an expression of "the basest sort of human depravity."[4]

The fatal flaw of "just war" theory is that people battling one another usually believe their cause is just. Wesley rightly observed that whatever "conspiracies" and "rebellions" may be used to justify the use of arms, the ensuing wars are always marked by "murders, massacres, avarice, faction, hypocrisy, perfidiousness [disloyalty], cruelty, rage, madness, hatred, envy, lust, malice, and ambition."[5] These are hardly activities that accord with the experience of a heart made perfect in love.

Conflicting Loyalties

"War is evil," says President Jimmy Carter, "but sometimes a necessary evil." When Dietrich Bonhoeffer became fully aware of Hitler's diabolical character, egomaniacal ambitions, and systematic extermination of the Jews, he abandoned the pacifism he had advocated so forcefully in his theological and devotional classic, *The Cost of Discipleship*, and joined a small group of high German officials committed to eliminating the Fuehrer. Because of his role in the failed plot, he was hanged 10 days before the Allies liberated Berlin. He is rightly revered as a Protestant martyr-saint.

Countless believers have had to make Bonhoeffer's hard choice between the lesser of two evils: either to let vicious warmongers and rogue nations destroy people and property at will, or do whatever is necessary to stop them.

If the United States, for instance, had intervened in the Rwandan war of genocidal self-destruction in 1994, hundreds of thousands of human lives might have been saved.

Neither Jesus nor Peter required that believing Roman centurions resign their military commissions. Paul acknowledged that "governing authorities" had been "established" by God, and that they exercise a positive role in protecting their citizens from dangerous felons within and violent aggressors from without (Romans 13:1-7). Indeed, we owe an enormous debt to those who have laid down their lives for the sake of our country, and those who, like my own son, continue to put their lives on the line to protect the incredible freedoms we enjoy. At the same time, we ought to respect those who for the sake of their religious convictions declare themselves to be conscientious objectors.

Where Is God in Times of War?

Elie Wiesel tells the horror story of being forced to watch, along with several thousand other Auschwitz death camp inmates, the hanging of 30 prisoners in retaliation for 3 that had escaped. One was a 10-year-old Dutch boy. His emaciated little body was so light that he twitched on the end of his rope for half an hour before expiring. Someone whispered, "Where's God in all this?" Someone else responded, "There! There he is, on the gallows!"

Whatever else happened when Jesus plumbed the depths of God-forsakenness on the Cross, we see that there is no black hole of violence or suffering where God in Christ is not present. Such it was for Kim Phuc, the Vietnamese girl enveloped in flames whose picture was beamed around the world. Nick Ut, the photographer, rushed her to a South Vietnamese hospital. Surprisingly, she survived even though over half of her body was covered with third-degree burns. She then spent 14 months at an American hospital in Saigon undergoing dozens of operations and therapy, her care paid for by a private foundation. Against all odds, she eventually returned to her village where she and her family began to rebuild their lives.

After the fall of Saigon, however, she was forced to leave school and abandon her dreams of becoming a doctor, and was sent to Ho Chi Minh City. There she was exploited by the Communist government for propaganda purposes. Deprived of family and friends, and sure that no man would ever marry her because of her disfigured body, she became so depressed that she wanted to die. It was during this desolate time that she came upon a New Testament in a library. She was deeply moved by the story of Jesus. At Christmas time in 1982, she invited Christ into her heart, and became a fervent believer.

Nevertheless, there remained a pocket of bitterness in her heart, anger at the Americans who had caused her so much pain and ruined her life—that is, until she read Jesus' call to "Love your enemies, do good to those who hate you" (Luke 6:27). For months those words haunted her. She kept telling herself that it was impossible to forgive. Gradually, however, her heart softened. She now testifies that "one day God's love set me free from hatred."[6] The change this brought was dramatic.

Four years later, she seized an opportunity to study in Cuba. There she met and married a fellow Vietnamese student. They spent their honeymoon in Moscow. On the trip back to Cuba, their airliner refueled in Gander, Newfoundland. They walked off, and were granted asylum by the Canadian government. They were cared for by Quakers, and eventually became Canadian citizens.

In 1996, the Vietnam Veterans Memorial Fund invited Kim to speak before several thousand Vietnam War veterans. It was there that she met the pilot who coordinated the air strike on her village, and was able to assure him of her forgiveness in person. Out of this experience grew the Kim Foundation, dedicated to helping children victimized by war around the world.

Today, Kim lives with her husband and two sons in the Toronto area where she works with the disabled. In 1997 UNESCO named her a Goodwill Ambassador for Peace. She travels widely, telling her story and testifying to the peace and forgiveness she has found in Jesus.

Scripture Cited: Genesis 1:31; Exodus 15:3, 6-7; 22:21-22, 24, 31; Psalms 7:9; 55:8; Isaiah 9:6; 13:3-16; 42:2-3; Matthew 1:23; 5:9, 38-48; 24:6; 26:52; Luke 6:27-36; 9:55; 23:34; Romans 3:23; 5:12; 6:23; 12:14, 21; 13:1-7; 15:33; Ephesians 6:12; Philippians 4:9; 1 Thessalonians 5:23; 2 Thessalonians 3:16; James 4:1-2; Hebrews 13:20; 1 Peter 2:21, 23; Revelation 21:1, 4

About the Author: Dr. Cowles is a professor at Point Loma Nazarene University in San Diego, California.

CHAPTER 3

When Different Religions Claim to Be True

by Joseph Coleson

MIKE AND ANN GREW UP in a small town in the upper Midwest of the United States. They attended the same church, were involved in its youth group, and went to the same high school. They started dating just before their junior year, after spending three weeks together on a youth group mission trip to Central America.

Ann's mother helped her plan the perfect June wedding in their church, and Mike walked down the aisle to his lovely bride three weeks after they received their diplomas, both with honors. Both were determined to acquire a higher education. Ann wanted to teach junior high English. Mike wanted to teach, too, but he didn't yet know what. The only thing that really punched his buttons was coaching cross country and track.

Mike and Ann decided they wanted the lower costs of attending the state university only an hour-and-a-half from home, instead of their denominational college three states away. Within two weeks of arriving on campus, they found a church and a Christian student group on campus, and began to feel settled in as they learned their way around campus and around town.

Settled, that is, until the semester really got going in

the comparative religions class they both were taking to fulfill a general education requirement. One night just before the first unit test, over the Chinese takeout they allowed themselves as their once-a-week treat, Ann observed plaintively, "We haven't even gotten to any of the religions that claim there are many gods, and already I'm wondering how we can know Christianity is the right one. I mean, are we Christians just because that's what we were born into? Besides, we see the other religious student groups doing pretty much what ours is doing. They do good things, they study their scriptures, they seem to lead moral lives, and they seem to have a pretty good time. Does it really matter what brand our religion is? I never thought about it back home, because everybody's a Christian in our little town—at least they wouldn't claim to be anything else. How can we know, anyway?"

Does It Really Matter?

Most monotheistic (belief in one god) and polytheistic (belief in many gods) faith and philosophical systems claim that it really doesn't matter what we believe. Some say no gods exist, and death is the end—period. Some say a few or many gods exist, or that God is within us all, and all paths will lead to heaven eventually, except maybe for the handful of persons who have stood out in history for their extreme evil.

The Hebrew/Israelite faith and its historical descendents—rabbinic Judaism, Christianity, and Islam—claim there is only one God. Judaism and Christianity teach that God is the self-revealed Transcendent Creator and Sovereign Lord of the universe. Whether Islam worships the same God as the other two faiths is debated—within, among, and outside the three monotheistic faiths.

The biblical record makes no attempt to prove the existence of a single God. It accepts God's existence as fact, and proceeds to tell the story of God's acts in creation and in redemption. That story, in all its many facets, seems to expect seekers to come to sufficient understanding that they can reasonably place their trust in God as the faithful Creator and Redeemer who will, as promised, bring us to eternal life. This final decision is a step of faith, just as trusting any human person is an act of faith we all exercise hundreds of times every day, without even thinking about it.

If what the Hebrew/Christian Scriptures assert about all this is false or fictional, it does not matter. It is merely a very interesting story from antiquity, with much moral teaching value. If there is a chance such a God as portrayed in the Bible exists, however, it is worth our while to do some checking.

Before moving on, a note is in order. Whatever you and I may think of it, postmodernism is here to stay, for quite a long while yet, at least. And postmodernism is not all bad; it actually has taught us much that is good and beneficial. However, precisely here is one juncture where we must be careful of what the postmodern spirit could lead us to believe.

Postmodernism tends to affirm that everything is relative, and even that two or more contradictory positions can be held at the same time. Yet, if the Bible is giving us an accurate picture of God as Creator and Redeemer, then some things are absolute, and mutually exclusive positions are as impossible spiritually as they are in ancient Greek logic. If so, then what we believe about the spiritually "big-ticket items," really does matter.

If It Matters, How Can We Know?

We can't know whether the Bible and the Hebrew/ Christian traditions are telling us the truth on the big issues until we check out for ourselves what they regard as the big issues, and what they are trying to tell us about them.

The Bible says, first, that God is Creator. God is not created. Nothing created is God, or will be God. Everything is created by God, directly or indirectly. The Bible does not say how or when in the ways the physical sciences want to know. It just says God created and, as far as this earth is concerned, God created in order to have intimate fellowship with this earth's highest creation—humankind.

Still, humankind rejected that intimate relationship with God for which we were created. The first humans did it, and we have been doing it ever since. Amazingly, God did not give up on us, but spent the intervening years preparing for an astonishing invasion to win back the desire of God's heart—you and me. This invasion was not with armies of angels, as we probably would have done it. God came as a human baby, born of a young virgin mother, born in a cattle stable, and laid to sleep in a feeding trough.

Jesus ate, slept, grew, talked, studied, worked, played, and prayed just as you and I do. He died, as you and I probably will. In human terms, His death sentence was unjust; in Divine terms, His death redeemed us, which was why He came to this earth in the first place. But the staggering thing, the event that has convinced countless persons of every generation and nearly every place since, is that He did not stay buried. At least, the tomb was empty. Many have tried to explain that empty tomb apart from Jesus' resurrection. No one has succeeded; no one ever will succeed. If God did not raise Jesus from the dead as the New Testament claims in some way on nearly every page, then that empty tomb just outside the walls of Jerusalem has no explanation whatsoever.

Perhaps you and I should think of this chapter as a road that climbs a hill, then descends on the other side. With that last paragraph, we have reached the crest of the hill, and can see for a long way both backward and forward. Backward, we can see from where we have come, and can understand that back there the hill itself blocked our vision forward.

Now we are at the crest of the hill. Before us is the declaration that Jesus Christ is the Second Person of the Trinity, now the Incarnate One, God become human flesh. We can accept or reject that statement as God's unique truth, and Jesus himself as the Truth, as He claimed to be. If we do accept it, we can start down the hill forward, seeing the way ahead enough to know that the road leads to heaven and, whatever heaven may or may not be, it most certainly is life with God forever.

We also can choose to reject the possibility of God interacting so directly with the human race—and on this physical earth, besides. Many voices, both modern and postmodern, whisper that such a set of events is not spiritual enough. God couldn't have acted that way. It all has to be a metaphor for living good, clean, moral lives of self-improvement and service to others. If we choose that option, we will turn around and retrace our steps down the hill, backward.

From the crest of the hill, that astounding, audacious claim of God-with-us-in-the-flesh, God-condemned-to-die-but-raised-to-life-on-the-third-day, gives us a crystal-clear view of the other "roads." The crest of the hill lets us see why none of them leads to the one place worth going. Beyond the crest, the road becomes a causeway, bearing the traveler safely above and over the chasm of death which swallows all who try to go forward by another way. That causeway is Jesus; He, and He alone, is the Way.

This writer has lived and studied in contexts and cultures that reflect the broad spectrum of the Jewish and Muslim faiths. I've studied and taught at avowedly leftist/liberal institutions, as well as in extremely conservative settings. I've ministered across the range of Wesleyan-Holiness and other Methodist denominations and movements, and have ministered in Anglican, Lutheran, non-Calvinist and semi-Calvinist Baptist and Presbyterian, Roman Catholic, and even Unitarian Universalist settings. Among my colleagues in my student days and the students in my classes have been Mormons, Seventh-Day Adventists, secularists, agnostics, and atheists.

When I had spent several years sorting it all out, and realized that the crest of the hill (to return to our metaphor) is the incarnation, the life, death, and resurrection of Jesus, the Second Person of the Triune God, I became affixed to the Christian faith. I never left the faith I was born to, but that was the Truth by which it became firmly mine, and not just my heritage. It sounds too obvious when we say it this way, but this is the way we need to say it to make it our own: Jesus is the Person who makes the Christian faith unique. To be a Christian is not to believe in a religion or a moral system. To be a Christian is to put one's trust in Jesus, the Incarnate God, the crucified-buried-and-resurrected Messiah, Christ, Anointed One.

With that settled, with the confidence of that view from the crest of the hill, I can go into any setting without being afraid my faith will not measure up. It isn't my faith; it is God's existence and God's work of passionate love in Jesus rescuing us from death and all the other effects of sin. My faith is "merely" assessing honestly and with rigor the evidence God has provided, and coming to an honest conclusion.

A Few Caveats

Being humans in a not-yet-glorified state, we all need a few pertinent reminders—fairly short, perhaps, but probably repeatedly, as well:

1. *Our assessment of other truth claims must be against the measurement of the truth claims of the Bible* and of the family of faith which has followed biblical teaching and practice through the centuries, if we really are convinced of their truth. Not everything believed by the Church or by various denominations over the centuries is true. Not everything asserted in other faith systems or philosophical systems is false. Certain truth claims in other systems can be true, in one way or another, or even in several ways together. (Remember, postmodernism is not all bad!) Still, every truth

claim from any source must be compatible with the real, intended teaching of the Bible, in what it asserts to be true. This is not because the Bible is magic, but because in the total witness of the Bible, rightly understood, God has recorded the revelation of God's Self in Christ, and Christ is Truth personified in a way infinitely greater than human poets and their poetry presently can fathom or express.

2. *The Bible is not, and the Christian faith is not, primarily a set of propositions to be believed.* The Bible reveals, and the Christian faith teaches and practices, a relationship with God instituted by our acceptance of God's great work in Jesus on our behalf. As a natural consequence, there follows a relationship of loving integrity with fellow believers and, as far as possible, with nonbelievers who are, after all, God's children by creation. "Natural" does not mean "instinctive." There is much we must be taught.

3. *We must not be arrogant, but loving, when telling anyone about our experience of and on this Way of Christ.* This precious relationship and truth is not "ours." It is God's, first, last, and always; we have it only by God's gracious gifting. If the people with whom we talk don't know or understand, it isn't always from stubbornness or evil intent. To cite just one example, many people have had their capacity to trust God, or "religious people," severely damaged by the hypocrisy of Christians. God was patient with us. God is patient with others, and so should we be. The work of convincing people of God's truth is not ours anyway. That is the work of the Holy Spirit. Our assignment is to tell what God has done for us, and for the rest of the family of faith throughout history. We are called to tell the story, but we are under the divine mandate to tell it with the love of God holding absolute sway over our hearts and our minds.

4. "Christian denominations are necessarily bad." *That statement, when thought or uttered, is either a devilish lie, or a lazy, fallen-human excuse.* No denomination is either sinless or blameless, but most are made up of people who are in vari-

ous stages of learning what it means to love God with all our beings, and our neighbors as ourselves. Most denominations began from mixed motives, some righteous and some less than righteous. Still, most denominations are part of the vast witness through the ages to God's infinite love and grace.

Most denominations have people they can reach and minister to, and incorporate into the family of God, that no other denomination could reach, or they have local congregations that can reach people no other local congregation in that place is reaching. Rather than worrying that some Christian denominations don't understand all the truth of God that we do, we should thank God for their presence, their witness, and their ministry. If we want to pray that God help them to understand God's truth more completely, let us be sure to do it with genuine humility, remembering Jesus' proverb about the speck of dust and the plank in the eye (see Luke 6:42).

What, Then?

We can enter any situation confidently, lovingly, with humility in ourselves, but with trust in the perfect faithfulness of God who loves us, who saves us, who delights in us, who instructs and counsels us, and who waits with open arms to welcome us home. Our hope is not in theological or philosophical systems, though Christian theology is very important to help us to understand, to share, and to teach our hope. Our hope is in Jesus Christ, and our faith is first our love affair with Him. Loving Him, we will want always to know Him better, and that closer relationship and deeper knowledge of Him that He invites and encourages. "Come . . . learn from me" (Matthew 11:28-29).

Scripture Cited: Matthew 11:28-29; Luke 6:42; see also Luke 2:1-20; 23:44—24:12.

About the Author: Dr. Coleson is professor of Hebrew Scriptures at Nazarene Theological Seminary, Kansas City.

CHAPTER 4

When the Church Is Disappointing

by Phillip Stout

"HONEY!" SHE CALLED up the stairs to her son. "Time to get up! Time to get ready for church!"

No answer.

"Honey! Time to get up!"

More silence.

"Honey?"

"I'm not going!"

In a pleasant, but firm voice she replied, "Of course, you're going."

"No, I'm not!"

"Why would you say that, dear?"

"Because," he replied, "the church is full of hypocrites. I don't like them, and they don't like me. They treat me bad. I'm not going!"

Now Mom is more than firm. She's adamant. "You get up right now and get yourself dressed! You're going to church!"

"Give me one good reason why I should go."

"I'll give you two! First, I'm your mother and if I say you're going to church, then you're going to church. Second, you're the pastor!"

Hope, Anticipation, and Disappointment

All of us have been disappointed with the Church. Why is that such a big deal? Isn't life full of disappointments? Why does disappointment with the Church rise to such a level that people use words like "devastation" and "betrayal"? To understand this, we need to understand our hopes and expectations.

Disappointment is simply the result of unfulfilled expectations. It is the negative that follows the positive. Anticipation, expectation, and hope can be highly exhilarating experiences. Disappointment is that crushing blow that mocks our dreams.

Because disappointment results from unfulfilled expectations, it follows that the greater the expectation, the greater the potential for disappointment. If I go to a bad concert, I leave the concert saying, "I wasted an evening on a lousy concert." No big deal. But if I had anticipated the concert for three months and if people had told me the artists were fabulous, I would leave the concert saying, "What a disappointment."

If I had sponsored the concert, putting my time, energy, and reputation on the line and it turned out to be a bust, I'd be saying, "Never again!" Because the greater my investment, the greater my expectation. The greater my expectation, the greater my potential for disappointment.

The ones who suffer the most when the Church disappoints them are the people who invest the most. I know people who have invested decades in a church. Over those years, they gave enormously of their time, their money, their passion, and their selves. They sacrificed their own dreams for the future of the church. Imagine the devastation they felt when a new pastor came who was threatened by their leadership and their spiritual authority. Imagine the pain when they felt forced to leave.

There is more. Our deepest disappointments are experienced in the context of relationships. It only makes sense. Our greatest expectations are in relationships, and the relationships that hold the highest potential for love and intimacy hold the highest potential for disappointment.

In the church, we expect intimate, vital relationships. We believe it is the place where we will be loved, accepted, embraced, and appreciated. We share pivotal, spiritual experiences with other people, believing that those people will be lifelong friends. And not just friends. We call them "brothers" and "sisters" and say we are part of the same family. Because the church holds so much promise for close, intimate relationships, it also holds great potential for devastating disappointment.

What Is the Church?

How do we deal with these disappointments? First of all, we must understand the nature of the Church. The church of Jesus Christ came into being at the intersection of the divine and the human. In the second chapter of Acts (commonly referred to as the birth of the Church) the gift of the Holy Spirit was poured out on the believers. The Spirit of Jesus filled ordinary humans in a dramatic way. When this happened, some observers believed they were full of alcoholic spirits (Acts 2:13). That seemed much more plausible than the thought of God's Spirit filling them. We still struggle with that. We still look at the Church with all its contradictions and wonder at times if we really are the dwelling place of God.

Go into the break room where you work, and you will probably see an assortment of coffee mugs that get a lot of use. Among them are some pretty nasty looking mugs. Some of them are chipped around the top, have a couple of cracks in them, and have coffee stains on the inside. The one you use the most is the one that looks the worst. Yet, you don't throw it away. Why? Because it can still hold a pretty good cup of coffee. In fact, I've discovered that if you buy Hawaiian macadamia coffee and grind it just right, a chipped, cracked, stained cup can hold a *perfect* cup of coffee.

A damaged container can still hold a treasure.

Paul writes, "God . . . made his light shine in our hearts to give us the light of the knowledge of the glory of God in the face of Christ" (2 Corinthians 4:6). This description of the perfect gift is followed by a huge word that introduces the contradiction. The word "but." "*But* we have this treasure in jars of clay" (v. 7, emphasis added).

We must understand that God chose to place His perfection in chipped, cracked, stained people—"jars of clay." The hurts, the sins, and the regrets of our past do not preclude us from being the dwelling place of God. The Church is the mystical union of chipped, cracked, stained people who are filled with the Holy Spirit.

The Body of Christ

"Now you are the body of Christ, and each one of you is a part of it" (1 Corinthians 12:27). "And he is the head of the body" (Colossians 1:18).

I don't think that is a metaphor. I think the first-century believers took those words literally. They knew that Jesus had come in the flesh. They knew that the Spirit of Jesus had inhabited a human body. He used that body in specific, intentional ways. He spoke words of comfort and confrontation. He touched and healed. He taught us how to know the Father. Then He gave His life for us.

Before He left His disciples, He promised them that He would send His Spirit to live in them. The Spirit of Jesus now inhabits His people. We are His mouth. We are His hands. We are to lay down our lives for one another. We literally are the Body of Christ.

This understanding of the Church has enormous ramifications concerning our view of one another. If you are the dwelling place of His Spirit and the physical presence of Christ on earth, it matters greatly how I treat you and how close I hold you to myself.

The Church Is Messy

Relationships are messy. There is no important relationship in my life that does not require maintenance and, at times, some cleaning up. On an ongoing basis I have to forgive and be forgiven. This is true in all of our meaningful relationships. It is true in the Church. The Church is messy because relationships are messy.

Perhaps the biggest messes come from unrealistic and conflicting expectations. Remember, disappointment results when expectations are unfulfilled. Because the Church involves so many relationships, the number and variety of expectations makes disappointment a constant.

To understand this, we need to look no further than the role of the pastor. One of the greatest sources of stress for pastors is the impossibility of living up to expectations. Unrealistic expectations are often placed on pastors by themselves as well as by other people. Yet, what can be even more stressful are the conflicting expectations.

Most people want their pastor to be successful, but everyone defines success differently. Most people want their pastor to do a good job, but everyone has a different job description in mind. To complicate this issue, most of these expectations are never communicated; they are assumed. A person assumes that certain things must be accomplished by the pastor. The pastor is never told this because that person assumes that everyone would define the pastor's role in the same way. When the pastor, who may have a completely different concept of pastoral ministry, does not live up to that person's expectations, disappointment results. Because that person still assumes the pastor views ministry in the same way he or she does, the next assumption is that the pastor must be lazy, undisciplined, or uncaring.

Conflicting expectations become a minefield for many pastors. Every time a pastor chooses to live up to one person's expectations, he or she is also choosing not to live up to another person's expectations, because those expectations are contradictory. Many pastors have left the ministry because of their disappointment over this very issue.

Now, if the expectations for the pastor can be so confusing, think about the expectations for the other leaders. They are even less defined. Then, there are the overarching expectations for the church in general. Many times people feel that they were not adequately cared for, they were abandoned in their time of need, they were judged unfairly—all of this, not by a person or a group of persons, but by the Church.

Lowering Our Expectations

To say that expectations must be realistic sounds a lot like saying you should lower your expectations. Is that the solution? Well, many have chosen that solution. Some have lowered their expectations to zero. They were so wounded that they left the Church, not just their local church, but the church of Jesus Christ. They are no longer a part of any group of believers. What they are saying is, "I have no expectations, so you can never disappoint me again."

It is a real tragedy when people use their disappointment as an excuse to be unfaithful to God. I am always astounded when I see people walk away from the Body of Christ after years of service and blessing. It is a strange logic that allows a person to say, "I have been disappointed by a human being, therefore I have no responsibility to God." Of course, logic has nothing to do with it. It is a lack of spiritual, emotional, and mental health that causes someone to destroy himself or herself spiritually because someone else did not live up to his or her expectations. They are not the only ones to suffer. Often their children end up spiritually malnourished in their formative years and never recover from it.

Others take a modified approach. They begin attending another church with the intention of living on the fringes. They decide that relationships are too messy, so they'll remain as anonymous as possible. A high level of investment creates too much potential for disappointment, so they'll stay on the receiving end instead of the serving end.

There is a problem with this approach. There doesn't seem to be any category for this type of believer in the New Testament. "Christ loved the church and gave himself up for her" (Ephesians 5:25). In our call to be like Jesus, we are not given two options: (1) You can give yourself to Christ and His body, or (2) you can give yourself to the Head and distance yourself from the Body.

The scriptures often compare our relationship with Christ to marriage. Imagine a young man with an engagement ring in his hand, kneeling before the woman he loves and saying, "I want to marry you. I love you. Well, not *all* of you. You see, I think your face is beautiful. I think your mind is brilliant. I guess what I'm saying is that I love your head. Your body, well, that's another story. I don't really like your body. I don't really want to be around it all that much. You I love. Your body—I could take it or leave it." Instead of sweeping her off her feet, he'd probably be picking himself up off the floor.

Imagine how offended Jesus must be when we tell Him we don't need or love His body. To be real Christ-followers, we don't have the option of taking it or leaving it. We have to take it. It is His body. He gave His life for it. He loves it. So to accept Him is to accept His body.

The Eternal in Here and Now

How do we keep our eyes on the beauty of the Body of Christ in the midst of great disappointment? It has a lot to do with focus. If I were to ask you to find something beautiful in your yard, you could do it. Because you were looking for it, your mind would be inclined toward beauty. You might bring me a flower or a plant, or it might simply be a blade of grass in which you had found beauty for the very first time. No matter how well trimmed or shaggy your lawn, you will be able to find beauty there.

The same would be true if I asked you to go in your yard and bring back some trash. When you're looking for trash, it is amazing how much you can find. I used to take a quick trip through the churchyard on Sunday mornings to pick up paper or rubbish that might have blown onto the lawn. I always intended to come back with one or two pieces of paper in my hand, toss them in the wastebasket, and go about my Sunday morning responsibilities. Yet without exception, I would find a lot of trash. I was always amazed at how many gum wrappers, broken sticks, paper cups, and bottles I would find. The lawn didn't look that bad when I went out. It was just that when I put my head down and looked for trash, I found plenty.

Now, come inside my church with me. Again, you will find what you're looking for. If you are looking for flaws, you will find them. If you are looking for sinners, you'll find them, because we welcome them with open arms. And if you're looking for the life-changing presence of the Holy Spirit, that is exactly what you will find.

I'm not saying that we should be blind to our problems. Church leaders should be in a constant state of prayerful evaluation of the local church. I'm not saying that we should ignore sin. Paul says that sin must be confronted—especially when it occurs in the leadership of the church. I simply want to remind us that when we're cleaning up the messes, we must do so with a lot of grace. And we must do so without losing sight of the beauty of Christ's presence in and among us.

The most common, and most dangerous, focus problem is the inward focus. Now, repeat these words after me: "It's not about me! It's not about me!" The Church is not on this earth to please me. The ministry of the local church should not be tailored to keep believers in their comfort zone. It doesn't matter if we use the kind of music that I would have chosen. It doesn't matter if the dress code bothers me. What matters is the mission of the Church.

Jesus gave us a vision for an aggressive Church, a Church that would withstand the gates of hell (Matthew 16:18). He commissioned us to take the gospel to all the nations on earth (28:19). And He promised that He would be with us, sustaining us, during the whole time (v. 20).

All of us together now (especially my fellow pastors): "It's not about me! It's not about me!"

Disappointment Happens

We are not the first to experience disappointment in the Church. Immediately after the birth of the Church in the 2nd chapter of Acts, we began to have our problems. In the 5th chapter, we find sin in the Church. In the 6th chapter, there were complaints that the leadership was not caring for everyone equitably (there were even hints of racism). In the 15th chapter, the two most influential leaders, Barnabas and Paul, "had such a sharp disagreement that they parted company" (v. 39). And that was the small stuff. This all came after a huge struggle to understand the calling of the Church (vv. 1-35). And to top it off, at the very outset, one of their most loved leaders had been murdered (7:54-59). Why would God let that happen?

That's a question I've heard before. "Why would God let that happen?" After all, we're trying to do His will. This is His church, not ours.

I don't understand why Jesus would entrust His message to you and me. We're so weak and selfish. We're so human. And yet, that is His design. I have to trust that the heart of Jesus can be communicated through the hearts of Jesus' followers. Paul said He chose to put His treasure in jars of clay "to show that this all-surpassing power is from God and not from us" (2 Corinthians 4:7).

My childhood, my adolescence, and my adult life have been lived in church. I've been a follower and a leader. I've seen it all. I have been disappointed by clergy and laypeople. I have been disappointed by institutions within the Church. I have seen godly people lose faith and lose their souls. I have seen the worst the Church has to offer.

I've also seen the best. In the Church, I have met the most noble, courageous people that God ever created. In the Church, I have received unconditional love. I have been the recipient of the Church's patience and understanding. In the Church, I have found leaders that I can respect and admire. It has become my family, and I am astounded that God loved me enough to give me the privilege of being part of His body.

Scripture Cited: Matthew 16:18; 28:19-20; Acts 2:13; 5—6; 7:54-59; 15:1-35, 39; 1 Corinthians 12:27; 2 Corinthians 4:6-7; Ephesians 5:25; Colossians 1:18

About the Author: Rev. Stout pastors the Church of the Nazarene in Jackson, Michigan.

CHAPTER 5

When Family Life Is Chaotic

by Cheryl Gochnauer

LYNN TENDS to get very calm in times of crisis. At this moment, she was nearly comatose.

Her 15-year-old daughter was perched on the couch with her equally delusional 16-year-old boyfriend, outlining their plans to get married on Valentine's Day. Not *some* Valentine's Day five years from now; Valentine's Day five *months* from now!

As Lynn listened to them fantasize as only teenagers can about living in her basement on ramen noodles and love, frantic prayers flew from her heart to heaven. Wasn't this the same strong-willed but sanctified girl she raised? The one who accepted Jesus in kindergarten? Who rededicated her life at junior high church camp? How many times had her mother and father talked frankly with her about purity and God's plan for her life?

Don't yell at them, she thought. *Be open. Be open. Be open!*

Immediately, another voice flashed inside Lynn's head, one she recognized from so many years walking with Jesus. *Get ready; here it comes.*

Lynn posed the question. "So, what is it? Do you want to get married simply so you can sleep together?"

"Oh, Mom," her daughter beamed. "We're already married in the eyes of God."

The conversation disintegrated from there.

Trapped

When they met in college, both Jason and Toni were active in Christian campus outreach. Though they often squabbled playfully, the attraction was strong. They made plans for the future, imagining God using them as missionaries in their workplaces while raising a family filled with love and affection.

The first year of marriage went relatively smooth. Sure, they got on each other's nerves sometimes, but they were smart, high-maintenance people, so that was normal, right?

Just give him a little space, and he'll get over it, she told herself.

Let her vent her feelings, and she'll cool off, he thought.

As time went by, however, a disturbing routine fell into place. His "space" turned into hours spent away from home. Letting her "vent" meant enduring screaming, accusations, and crying jags. Bickering and nitpicking shredded their relationship. Frantic prayers evolved into dubious demands, then bounced off the ceiling until both Jason and Toni stopped seeking God. Nothing seemed clear anymore.

Church activities that used to crowd their schedules dwindled as the couple became more disillusioned. When they did make it to a small group or a potluck, it felt like their smiles were painted on. Jaded thoughts pricked their consciences when the pastor or their small-group leaders taught about marriage. *'Til death do us part, huh? I'm so miserable that I'm ready to kill myself. For better or worse, I'm trapped.*

Violated

Kristie crushed her five-year-old son Michael against her chest as the room swayed. *Sweet Jesus! NO!* Her heart screamed while Michael tearfully described the sexual encounter with a middle-aged relative, and the innocence of her child's life was ripped away.

Kristie's hands shook as she dialed the authorities. In

the resulting firestorm of family division, police inquiries, and legal manueverings, agonizing questions plagued her: *How could God allow this evil to overtake her little boy? What happened to those guardian angels who were supposed to be watching over him?*

Rain or Shine

As Lynn, Jason and Toni, and Kristie have discovered, becoming a Christian doesn't shield us from heartbreak. We live in a fallen world, and our families are vulnerable to the same temptations and tragedies that plague those who haven't welcomed Christ into their lives. As Matthew 5:45 soberly reminds us, God "causes [the] sun to rise on the evil and the good, and sends rain on the righteous and the unrighteous."

We may dodge drops for a while, watching other families drown in the pain of divorce, devastating injury, or rebellious children. But eventually, trouble floods nearly every home.

This is nothing new. The Bible is full of stories of families on edge. In more than one case, people who were used to basking in God's sunlight questioned where He disappeared to as the clouds began rolling in.

Flesh of My Flesh

Prodigal children have been breaking the hearts of their mothers and fathers ever since Adam and Eve looked at the apple and said, "What does *He* know?" Teens and preteens are under more pressure than ever before to toss traditional values and forge ahead under their own steam. For Christian parents, the discovery that their child is involved in deception, drugs, alcohol, and/or sexual activity triggers a devastating realization: no matter how much love and morality you pour into an individual, free will reigns.

So why would God allow our children to drift away

from the faith? Because He is neither a tyrant nor a manipulator. Though He helps us to see the choices laid out before us more clearly, He allows each of us to draw near or pull away as we choose.

One reason it hurts so much to watch our children step off the narrow path is because many of us have experienced the repercussions of bad adolescent behavior ourselves. We know the kinds of trouble they can get into, and want to shield them from it.

A feeling of helplessness can set in as parents realize there is little they can do to moderate a determined teen's behavior. This is why it is so important to "train a child in the way he should go" (Proverbs 22:6), seeking God's direction and asking forgiveness for and rectifying inevitable parenting missteps along the way. In the dark days, everything you have invested in your prodigal will still be lying dormant inside, like a timed-release capsule God can use to help turn his or her heart toward home.

In the meantime, the emotional pain suffered by parents of prodigals can become overwhelming, interfering with work, friendships, and even physical health. Author and speaker Jeanette Gardner Littleton suggests that embattled parents:

Cut back on obligations. "Try to alleviate as much stress as you can," Littleton says. "Feel free to just say no to anything that will add more negative stress. Don't expect yourself to keep up with your normal pace."

Seek help from friends and professionals. Don't keep secrets. Confide in trusted friends who will offer up intercessory prayer for your family, and don't let a perceived stigma prevent you from talking with your doctor about medication to help during this difficult time. "Part of me felt like I'd failed spiritually because I couldn't just trust God and snap out of it," admits Karol, one of Littleton's interviewees. "But I had also read about brain chemistry and had learned stress can trigger chemicals that can cause de pression. And medication can be a means God uses to help us get chemicals in our body operating smoothly again."

Let go of what you can't control. "When we continually focus on our absent children," Littleton says, "we end up living in an up-and-down world—a continual cycle of hope and despair." Littleton reminds us that God knows exactly where the prodigal is, and His love is endless. Releasing a lost child into His hands is the best—and sometimes, the only—move a Christian parent can make.

Take care of yourself spiritually. Waiting for a positive outcome that may or may not come can take a toll on our spiritual health. "When we've been raised in our faith to cling to Bible promises and [believe] that God will answer our prayers, to so fervently turn to Him and not see His work can wear us out and discourage us," Littleton notes. Nevertheless, don't stop petitioning heaven. "We may not find the answers to all of our theological questions. Yet as we go to God with them, we will find a concerned Father who grieves with us. We'll find a God who loves our children much more than we ever could. And we'll find a Father who is also concerned about us."[1]

Till Divorce Do Us Part

Statistics regarding marriage and divorce paint a somber picture: In the United States, over one-third of all faith-based unions fail. If both husband and wife are Christians, why can't they get along without fighting?

Common reasons include immaturity, lack of communication skills, and focusing on the situation instead of the solution. When a couple refuses or doesn't know how to handle their differences of opinion in Christian ways, anger can become the prevailing atmosphere at home.

There are some concrete steps Christian couples can take to defuse conflict, however.

Do not let emotions rule. God gave emotions to bless us, not lead us. The "if it feels good, do it" attitude is deeply ingrained in our society, and our flash-fire responses to circumstances we don't like can quickly transport us to places in our marriage where we shouldn't be. James 3:6 describes the tongue as a fire, and emotions make perfect kindling. When a discussion begins escalating into an argument, *stop and step away from each other.* Take a timeout until both husband and wife can talk reasonably.

Be flexible. Christian couples should be steadfast in faith, but moveable in direction. When possible conflicts related to jobs, children, health, or some other major cataclysm appear, remain open with each other and discuss the options together. If you start arguing, see the paragraph above.

Worship together at home. It's tough to argue with someone you've just studied Scripture with or prayed over. Also, the Holy Spirit has a way of making applicable verses leap off the page when a couple is determined to work through their problems with God's help.

Say you are sorry. "I always admire people who are willing to look in the mirror, hold themselves accountable, have remorse for the things they've done wrong, and have the willingness to repair and not repeat their unpleasant actions," says Dr. Laura Schlessinger.[2] While Dr. Laura praises humility (as does the Sermon on the Mount), Jesus also reminds us in the Lord's Prayer that we will be forgiven as we have forgiven others.

Counseling can be helpful in providing communication tools and working through existing problems, but be careful when selecting a therapist. Colossians 2:8 warns, "See to it that no one takes you captive through hollow and deceptive philosophy, which depends on human tradition and the basic principles of this world rather than on Christ." That said, therapy can be a godsend to couples in conflict, as they learn practical ways to build or restore a Christian marriage.

In the Jaws of the Lion

Make no mistake: There really is a devil, and he really *is* out to get us. He is vicious, highly intelligent, devious beyond imagination, well-armed, and extremely patient. The Bible describes him like "a roaring lion, looking for someone to devour" (1 Peter 5:8). Some of his most heinous tools fall under the category of abuse—sexual, physical, and emotional.

Abuse seems to be happening everywhere—in schools, churches, and even in Christian homes. How is God available, or even recognizable, when a Christian family finds itself trapped in the jaws of abuse?

For those suffering the maltreatment, the anguish is often compounded by a belief that either God doesn't care, or He has allowed it to happen because they did something wrong. However, as Dr. James Dobson illustrates, "His heart is especially tender toward the downtrodden and the defeated. He knows your name and He has seen every tear you have shed. He was there on each occasion when life took a wrong turn. And what appears to be divine disinterest or cruelty is a misunderstanding at best and a satanic lie at worst."[3]

Instead of picking on the abused, God's Word promises dire consequences for the abuser, especially those who harm children: "It would be better for him to be thrown into the sea with a millstone tied around his neck than for him to cause one of these little ones to sin" (Luke 17:2).

"The serious and sincere student of the Bible will not escape these twin truths," says Josh McDowell. "God loves children, commands parents to love and nurture them, and will severely judge those who do them harm."

Parents can tear themselves up, wondering where those guardian angels were as their child was being abused. In response, Jesus acknowledges both the agony and the hope: "In this world you will have trouble. But take heart! I have overcome the world" (John 16:33).

McDowell also suggests several steps to help an abuse victim by showering him or her with understanding and God's love. Some highlights include:

Listen. Try to elicit all the facts without demanding all the details. Question him or her gently, and listen patiently before asking another question.

Empathize. Hurting people don't need instruction as much as they need someone to cry with, someone who will love them, and hurt with them.

Affirm. Sincere affirmation is one of the most therapeutic responses to a victim of abuse. Let him or her know that God loves him or her unconditionally and that you do too.

Direct. Help him or her acknowledge that God did not cause the abuse, but that He is the solution to the trauma caused by the abuse. Also help him or her accept the fact that healing will take time.[4]

Our lives are built on relationships, and none are more intimate than the family bonds—husband and wife and/or parent and child. It is within these relationships that we experience our highest highs and lowest lows.

So where is God when family life is chaotic? No matter how desperate our home situation may become, our Heavenly Father is right beside us, and His tears mingle with our own. He is an ever-present and faithful Friend, especially in times of trouble.

Scripture Cited: Proverbs 22:6; Matthew 5:45; Luke 17:2; John 16:33; Colossians 2:8; James 3:6; 1 Peter 5:8

About the Author: Cheryl Gochnauer is the founder of Homebodies <www.homebodies.org>, an on-line and print ministry for present and prospective at-home parents.

CHAPTER 6

When Divorce Happens

by Ellen Cox

JANET AND PAUL were a great couple. They were obviously devoted to one another. They had the same big plans for themselves and their future. It was no surprise, then, when they announced they were engaged. "A marriage made in heaven" could be, and was, applied to them.

So, it was with great anticipation and joy that friends and family participated in the planning of their wedding. Festive announcements were mailed far and wide. Just the right songs were picked out to convey Janet and Paul's love for each other. Beautiful rings were selected to symbolize their lifelong commitment. Scripture was read and vows were exchanged. Congratulations and gifts for the happy couple followed. It was a happy and typical wedding, and, indeed, this was a marriage made in heaven!

So, it was a shock when five years later, quiet news leaked out that Janet and Paul's marriage was over. How could this have happened? How could something so promising, so "perfect" in the beginning, end in the opposite way? And where was God in this?

Surprising Statistics

It may be surprising to the Christian community that statistics for divorce among couples professing to be born-again do not differ greatly from non-Christian couples.

George Barna, leader in evangelical poll-taking, finds that
a Christian marriage shows about a 34 percent likelihood
for divorce. This is only a 1 percent to 4 percent difference
from the non-Christian arena, where divorce stands at 35
percent to 38 percent. Barna also found that divorce rates
among conservative Christians were much higher than for
other faith groups.[1] Dr. James Dobson of *Focus on the Family*
reports there has been a 72 percent increase in the past
decade of households headed by unmarried partners.[2] This
increase might indicate that too much trust has been
placed in the idea that because a couple is Christian, they
will somehow be immune to divorce. The alarming trend
highlights the fact that churches may not be doing all they
can to minister to families.

The Path of Divorce

The question should be asked, then, what leads a
born-again Christian couple down this road to divorce? In
all marriages, there are endless reasons for a dissolution.
For some, a drifting apart has occurred. As they each got
older, interests and goals changed. What was once a shared
dream became separate ideals. They lost the connection
somewhere along the way.

Another reason is a shift in priorities. What was once
important was exchanged for a new set of priorities. The
day-to-day pressures and demands of living got in the way
or created a wedge. Whatever the cause of the shift, the
emphasis on staying a healthy couple was moved to a
place of lesser importance.

It could be that passion was mistaken for love. Many
times, the power and allure of attraction is so strong, the
couple simply becomes blind to the fact that genuine love is
not present. This is a dangerous trap. It often leads to trouble when, "after the honeymoon is over," problems begin to
arise, with no real foundation to help stabilize the marriage.

Maybe dissatisfaction with the marriage developed,

and an affair was initiated. Seldom is an affair about wanting a new marriage, but a case of the "greener grass" syndrome. Somehow, something else looks better than what is currently available, so sin enters the picture and dissolves the marriage.

For example, Susan's relationship with Todd began to grow stale. She struck up a friendship with a coworker, which soon led to romance. She would tell her lover things she had long ago stopped telling Todd. In time, the affair ended, but the damage was done and the marriage soon dissolved. The "greener grass" wasn't as green as she'd thought.

What needs to be understood is that there is no such thing as "a marriage made in heaven." To expect a marriage with no problems or difficulties is a myth—a dangerous one that leads couples to ignore the warning signs. It is no guarantee that, just because a marriage can be defined as a Christian one, problems won't arise and incorrect choices made. To expect otherwise is to expect a fairy tale.

What Is the Biblical Marriage?

Probably no one would disagree with the fact that God wants permanent marriages. Any other option is less than His plan. Dr. Alex Deasley, in his book *Marriage and Divorce in the Bible and the Church,* supports this when he said, "Marriage is grounded, not in casual alliance based on attraction or passing convenience, but on covenant commitment implying faithfulness and permanence."[3] In Genesis, God outlined His plan for marriage as a partnership and completion of two individuals.[4] Jesus reaffirmed this plan in Mark 10:8-9 when He said, "They are no longer two, but one. Therefore what God has joined together, let man not separate."[5] His ideal for marriage and its permanency was used to help Israel and the rest of us understand God's irrevocable covenant of faithfulness. Israel's fickle heart was famous, but God was bound by His love and covenant to faithfulness in the face of her wandering allegiance.[6]

Deasley cautions us to understand, however, that God's use of the marriage illustration is to help us understand God's contract with humanity. To apply God's perfection to human imperfection would be an injustice. God took into account human imperfection when He allowed for divorce on the grounds of adultery. This isn't disputed. Yet, the question arises: What then is an acceptable reason for divorce?

Obviously adultery is addressed, but would we "hard-line" the subject and say a battered spouse must remain in a destructive and dangerous marriage? The argument is made that the abusive partner may come to repentance and change through continuing the marriage. To this, Jesus' own arguments in the Sermon on the Mount (Matthew 5—7) for the honoring of the spirit of the Law and not the letter of the Law comes into play. The health and safety of one of the partners is not required on the sacrificial altar of marriage permanence. The very act of the Genesis marriage was based on creation of equal partnership for the health and growth of the other.[7] It can be concluded, then, that if this is in jeopardy for one partner, then the marriage has ceased its primary function. So, the question of acceptability must always be examined under the two goals of God: His desire for faithful covenant and His desire for devotion to the spirit of the Law.

The Third Partner

The reality of things is that the rise in divorce among Christian couples brings with it the question of what role the Church plays. There are two areas in which the Church completes its own function in a couple's marriage. The first area is *proactive,* the second is *reactive.*

One could logically look at the fact that the Church is an active participant in the marriage ceremony. Therefore, it is logical that it would play as a participant in the marriage as well. No one would support the idea of watching the union celebration, then giving a collective slap on the back and a hearty "good luck." The Church's participation continues beyond that. It starts with the preparation before marriage. Premarital counseling is a must for couples. It acts as the initiation of the couple into open, honest dialogue that will continue through the course of the marriage. To go into a union without at least basic counseling is akin to throwing someone into deep water without first teaching him or her to swim. Going through the course of premarital counseling allows the Church, by way of the pastor or counselor, to have an opportunity to address the red flags of a relationship or even advise against it, if necessary.

Another aspect of proactive church involvement would be post-marriage enrichment. The idea that the backbone of our society is the health of its marriages is of paramount importance. The models that we display of covenant to our children teach them about more than just a marriage, it teaches about commitment to values and to each other. If our vows and promises are soluble, upon what foundation do they have to build? If the Church doesn't take active measures to help marriages succeed, we fail not just the couple, but also the generations that follow.

Programs specifically directed for the enrichment of marriages should be emphasized, resources should be made available for couples' use, and mentoring programs established for the newly married couples for the first year. Finally, intervention when divorce seems to be the coming result should take place.

An example of this would be Steven. His friends knew of the temptation to have an affair, so they made plans to intervene. Steven's friends increased contact with him. They began to show up where Steven might be alone. In a sense, they hounded Steven, and essentially made it impossible for him to get into a favorable position for an affair.

The moral of this is to be nosy to some extent; be willing to be involved in the lives of fellow brothers and sisters.

When it is obvious that a marriage is in trouble, make every effort to give encouragement for the couple to seek Christian marriage counseling. The aspect of *Christian* counseling is important, because a worldly view of marriage cannot be allowed to dictate the course of a marriage or its healing. The fact is that every marriage needs help at some point in some ways, whether or not that includes professional counseling. The Church needs to make certain that it is fulfilling its role in the marriage.

After the Fact

The second role the Church plays is reactive. After a divorce has happened, the Church has a responsibility to help the now two separate individuals rebuild their lives. The average person has connections to someone—either friends or family—who have been through a divorce. Divorce, sadly, has affected every one of us. When divorce happens, it isn't just a loss between a husband and wife and their families, it is a loss to the church community as well. To help those heal who are going through it is to help the church community heal also.

If the decision is mutual, there are two people who are hurting and need help during the process. They are on unfamiliar ground with crushing emotions and pressures. Both sides need to be supported. They need help in practical areas, the first being fellowship. Don't avoid them. Because we don't know how to help or even react to the divorce, the initial response may be to avoid altogether those involved. This is detrimental to their healing and restoration. Such course of action only leads to discouragement and feelings of abandonment, compounding the feelings they are already having at the dissolution of their marriage.

Another avenue of practical help is financial assistance. Money might be an issue, and the Body must step in to take care of basic needs that arise. This can range from groceries and gas to house payments. Sensitivity on the Church's part is needed and valued.

Loneliness will be a heavy emotion. Frequent phone calls, visits, and company need to be made to keep the individuals connected. Feelings of loss will be present. The feelings of loss won't be limited to just the loss of a spouse or marriage. Depending on the circumstances, there may be a limited amount of time with children. Family members will experience these losses too. Support groups should be developed to give the individuals a chance to talk and experience group fellowship. There will be a need for rebuilding an identity as an individual rather than as part of a couple. Counseling, as well as the support of others who have been through the same experience, can help here.

The self-esteem of those involved will take a heavy hit. Feelings of failure and a fear of rejection among their old social circles are sure to hound them. Again, not only the Church's expression of sorrow at the ending of their marriage, but also a firm acceptance and love for them, is required and needs to be demonstrated at every opportunity.

Another troubling aspect of divorce is bitterness. There is no greater emotion that is so devastating and poisoning to a person's relationships than bitterness. When it takes root, it slowly destroys the person, his or her relationships with others, and his or her relationship with God. It isn't always the divorced that fights this battle. Parents seeing their hurting children often face this challenge of forgiving the "offending partner."

Maggie had a close relationship with her daughter-in-law when Sharon broke the news that she was leaving her son. Seeing her son hurting so much caused such bitterness that it began to affect Maggie's relationship with God. She began to pray daily for help in forgiving Sharon, but it wasn't until she confided with a pastor concerning her struggles that she began to make headway with overcoming her bitterness.

Children can become bitter and angry at parents and will strike out at those around them. No significant healing can occur when bitterness has taken hold. The Church can help in effective ways by lifting those involved in prayer, through encouragement, and lending a listening ear through support groups or personal individual contact.

Perhaps one of the greatest ways the Church can serve as God's comforting and healing hand is by helping the children affected by divorce. To assume that kids are resilient and they will "get over it" is to blind ourselves to the truth. On their web site, *Focus on the Family* reported findings by Dr. Judith Wallerstein, an authority on children and divorce. It was her finding that 37 percent of children of divorce "were even more unhappy and dissatisfied five years after the divorce than they had been eighteen months [after the divorce]."[8] She has found in her 25 years of study that 40 percent of her subjects never married. This is a drastic difference when compared to her study that showed only 16 percent of children from intact families never married.[9] Dennis Rainey stated that children from divorced homes are four times more likely to commit a violent crime. It increases the "likelihood of a child living in poverty, dropping out of school, and becoming a juvenile delinquent."[10] Clearly, divorce profoundly affects the children for the rest of their lives.

When divorce is a reality, we must step in as the Church and support the children as well as the parent. If kids don't have a strong foundation when they are growing up, they don't grow up to give one to their children. Our society has been shaken to its core with unstable marriages and homes. This is a key reason we must do all we can as a church to come alongside couples, both before a divorce as well as after one.

God's Promised Future

As stated before, anything less than a permanent, healthy marriage is less than God's plan for His people— but we don't always follow that perfect plan. However, God established the Church through His Son, and individuals can partner with each other, help one another, encourage one another, support one another, and hold each other accountable. When one person stumbles, the Church collectively should be rushing to aid. When one part of the Body falls, everyone feels the impact.

God cares through it all. A divorce does not divorce people from God. Romans 8:38 says, "I am convinced that nothing can ever separate us from his love. Death can't and life can't. The angels can't and the demons can't. Our fears for today, our worries for tomorrow, and even the powers of hell can't keep God's love away. Whether we are high above the sky or in the deepest ocean, nothing in all creation will ever be able to separate us from the love of God that is revealed in Christ Jesus our Lord" (NLT). This is a clear statement. God is faithful and present. He doesn't leave or forsake us. The choices that we make affect the course and direction our lives take. Sometimes those choices involve sin that needs to be confessed and forgiven, but His love and acceptance is constantly available.

Whether a person finds himself or herself the innocent and unwilling participant in a divorce or the initiator, God is there to be found. He doesn't make himself hard to find. Believers can trust the truth of God's Word and faithfulness, even when circumstances seem to crush them. God can forgive, and life can move forward. His grace is usually looking forward, while people tend to look back. Jeremiah 29:11 states, "'For I know the plans I have for you,' declares the LORD, 'plans to prosper you and not to harm you, plans to give you hope and a future.'" God's vision and plan for the lives of those who trust Him is not so small that He can't use anything to make a future for them.

God's hand is everywhere to be seen, if people will just ask for eyes to see Him. The trials of individuals' lives have been eloquently compared to a tapestry of which we only see the knotted and tangled underside. This is a wonderfully accurate illustration of the complete masterpiece that God is creating, even out of the biggest heartbreaks. However, whenever the Church steps in to help each other, a wonderful chance to glimpse the other side of that tapestry is given.

Scripture Cited: Jeremiah 29:11; Matthew 5—7; Mark 10:8-9; Romans 8:38

About the Author: Ellen Cox is a freelance writer, living in Topeka, Kansas.

CHAPTER 7

In Addictions

by Paul Fitzgerald

SHERRI* GLANCED at her watch. She was surprised that her group had been meeting for more than an hour. Her fear that nobody would understand her story was gone. She had questioned if anyone could understand what she had been through. Now she sensed that this was the right place for her. The group respected her silence. Most had been coming only a few months and recalled their fear in that first meeting.

June continued her response to the question, "The last time you encountered an angry or critical person (for example, spouse, boss, friend), how did you find yourself reacting?" She experienced overwhelming fear whenever her husband exploded in a rage in front of the children. His compulsive pattern of anger with authority figures had led to trouble at work again. They had moved from their hometown where he had lost several jobs over his rage. She was afraid it was happening all over again.

Bob shared about his fear of facing his wife in their first family session at the hospital, where she was in addiction treatment. A nurse, she struggled with addiction to prescription drugs. She had tried to stop on her own, but it never lasted long. Life had finally become unbearable for Bob and their teenage children. He had arranged with a therapist, their pastor, and a few friends for an intervention. Together, they had confronted her with specific incidents where her addictive behavior had hurt them. She had agreed to be admitted for treatment, but angrily told

Bob she felt abandoned and betrayed. Bob was not sure she would ever want to see him again.

Sherri heard other members share how afraid they were of alcoholic spouses who threatened them. She recognized the stories so similar to her own. Her unconscious nodding became a rocking motion of her whole body. She began sobbing quietly, and the group waited in silence. She pulled a tissue from her purse. "I'm sorry. I really didn't mean to cry like this."

June spoke up immediately, "That's all right, honey. In this group, it's safe to feel anything. You can tell us as much or as little as you want."

Sherri responded to the opening and told them how afraid she had been to come to the meeting. "I have prayed to God for years to help pull my husband out of alcoholism, but it has only gotten worse. My sister keeps telling me to leave him, but I haven't been able to do that. I am his only connection to the church. Where is God in all this mess?"

The group was nodding in recognition of her story. They had lived through similar experiences and had asked the same questions: How can you help an addicted spouse? What does a Christian do to help an addicted spouse? What can the Church do to help us? Does God really love me?

Anxious Responses to Addiction

Ask the spouses of those addicted to alcohol, drugs, work, spending, gambling, food, sex, etc., and they can name what does not work. They have tried pretending that the problem was not addiction. They have covered up and made excuses, hoping it would go away. They have taken on the full responsibility for the household and family. They have tried to control the finances and have tried being constantly with the addicts to control their choices. They have nagged, threatened, yelled at them, hidden money, cried, and threatened to leave. Over time, these efforts take a toll emotionally and spiritually. They become exhausted, depressed, and despair of finding any help. It seems that even God has abandoned them.

These are just a few of the anxious responses to the anxiety presented by their spouses' addictive choices. Addictions have complex physical, emotional, and spiritual causes. Addictive use of a substance or a process (e.g., gambling, spending) begins as a way of coping with problems that seem overwhelming. The relief is temporary but the result is increased anxiety, which is brought home and dumped on the family. The family's anxious response to their behavior confirms the addict's fears. A vicious cycle of increasingly anxious responses begins which can quickly reach the point of explosion. A habitual communication pattern develops in which each person comes to know where the anxious exchanges will end, even before they begin. Everyone is doing something, but none of it leads to recovery.

Emotional and Physical Cutoff Response

An alternative response to the stress of life with an addict is an emotional and physical cutoff of contact with the addict. After all the anxious responses have failed, a cutoff may seem to be the only option left. The family becomes emotionally exhausted. The thought of more efforts to change the addict and the fear of failure is overwhelming. Spouses feel driven to an emotional and physical cutoff when their anger and exhaustion exceeds their fear of being alone.

Leaving the addict's physical presence because of physical, emotional, or sexual abuse is always an appropriate choice. Everyone has the right to protection from abusive behavior. Children must be protected from the risk of abuse. In the absence of abuse, a spouse may suddenly switch from anxious responses to a cutoff of emotional or physical presence as self-protection from the addict's anxiety. A cutoff may provide an immediate escape for the family, but it usually leaves the addict more anxious and feeling abandoned. Relief for the family may be short-lived as well. New challenges and choices must be faced, for which they may be emotionally, physically, and spiritually unprepared.

The Response of Nonanxious Emotional Presence

Remaining emotionally present yet choosing nonanxious responses to the addict's behavior is challenging. The support of others who have been through similar experiences is critical to avoid falling back into anxious responses or cutoffs as the addiction worsens. This response requires finding a healthy spirituality that affirms the dignity of choice for the addict's family members, puts responsibility on the addict to choose to pursue recovery or not, and recognizes God at work in the painful process. Following are the steps to adopting the response of nonanxious emotional presence.

1. Accept that the problem exists. It is usually difficult for family and friends to accept that the term "addict" describes the compulsive behaviors of a loved one. The person may be effectively functioning in some areas of life, while failing in others. Forget the stereotype of an addict as someone lying in a gutter. Addicts more often than not look like everyone else.

The addicted person is the last one to accept that a problem exists. His or her defense mechanism of denial appears as obvious lying to everyone else, but it allows the addict to not see what would be too painful to admit. Addicts learn to evade any mention of the addiction and problems resulting from their choices. They shift the focus to other people and problems that become the "real rea-

son" for their problems. They shift blame outside themselves for their addictive choices.

Adults and children who live with an addict are negatively affected by that relationship. The addict's ability to
deny that his or her problem exists or to shift the blame, often to the spouse, may be so effective that others accept
blame. Life with an addict has been described as "crazy-
making." Obviously painful behavior is denied as if it did
not exist. Family members may come to doubt their own
sanity. The effects of living with an addict can be very serious, requiring a recovery process separate from the addict's recovery. The term most often used to describe the
result of living with an addict is "codependency."

Acceptance that the problem exists is the first step in
helping the addict. The family's admission of the problem
cannot wait on the addict's acceptance that the problem exists. Acceptance requires breaking free of the denial and
blaming used by the addict. It requires breaking the silence
and talking to someone about the experience of living with
the addict. The goal is not to find someone to fix the problem, but others with whom reality can be tested to avoid being pulled back into denial. Hopefully, it will be possible to
talk confidentially to a pastor knowledgeable about addictions, who will encourage and support the recovery process.

2. Educate yourself about addiction. If a spouse or child was
diagnosed with a rare disease, most of us would ask questions and go to the Internet to find out all we could about the
condition and how to treat it. The same approach holds for
addictions. There are many myths about addiction that are
widely accepted, but have no basis in reality. In recent years,
helpful books on addiction and the effects of living with an
addict are easily found, even in Christian bookstores.

Libraries have references for national organizations
for recovery of specific addictions (e.g., Alcoholics Anonymous, Overeaters Anonymous, Gamblers Anonymous)
that offer toll-free numbers to call for free literature. They

also have lists of local chapters in most communities that offer information and support. In the last decade, many churches have begun recovery ministries that offer information and support in the context of the church. (The National Association for Christian Recovery is a fellowship of Christians who identify themselves as being in recovery and maintain a national directory of clergy and counselors knowledgeable about recovery.)

3. *Take the steps of healthy spiritual surrender.* Recovery from addictions and from the effects of living with an addict is at its heart a spiritual process. There are many examples where the cycle of addiction has been immediately broken in a crisis spiritual experience. More often, recovery requires a spiritually healing process in addition to a single crisis experience.

The Twelve Steps of Alcoholics Anonymous has proven to be one effective tool for the process of recovery. The Steps can and have been adapted into a specifically Christian context to counter many kinds of addictions and compulsive behaviors. Here we have presented an adaptation of the first three Steps suggesting how the addict's spouse may begin the process of recovery.

Step One "We admitted we were powerless over our addicted loved one; that our lives had become unmanageable."

This Step requires acceptance that no one can change another who does not want to change. It also requires honesty about the consequences of living with an addict. As addictions progressively worsen over time, the chaos felt by family and friends increases. This is not giving up on the addict, but it is giving up on trying to be powerful enough to change them. It accepts our "powerlessness" over the choices of others, yet does not deny our responsibility of making healthy choices in our situation.

Step Two "Came to believe that God could restore us to sanity."

This Step implies that past choices have not been in the best interest of ourselves or our loved ones. Acknowledging that may feel strange since we have tried to do the best we knew. Often there is a pattern of doing the same things over and over, expecting but not seeing the desired results.

This Step shows clearly that the move from addiction to recovery must be a God-directed process. Where we are weak and ineffective to conquer addictions, God is adequate, willing, and already working to restore individuals and families to a state of relationship with Him and with each other.

Step Three "Made a decision to turn our will and our lives over to the care of God."

This is often the first step claimed by both the addict and spouse when things are at their worst. Sometimes it seems as though the decision is taken back when things improve. The challenge of this step is to really turn over the results of turning over life and will to God. Everyone is ready at times to turn over life when it seems out of control, but we do so assuming it will turn out the way we want. Admitting our "powerlessness" in the first step prepares for this step and truly letting go of the results to God. Recovery can not be truly effective without acknowledging our weakness, our sinfulness, our repentance, our faith, and—most of all—His grace.

These are basic steps in a spiritual formation process that embraces God as both emotionally present and a source of nonanxiety. Scripture suggests that God desires an emotionally intimate relationship with His people (e.g., Psalms 131; 139). Other passages identify God as being like a nonanxious Rock, Strong Tower, and Fortress for His people (e.g., Psalms 18; 31; 62). Jesus' teaching in the Sermon on the Mount (Matthew 5—7) centers on God's strength and stability becoming the source of the ability to make nonanxious choices in anxious situations. Romans

12:9-21, 15:1-5, and Philippians 4:4-9 are just a few examples where believers are challenged to make nonanxious choices. Both Romans 8:26-28 and James 1:2-4 proclaim that God is actively involved in the lives of people through both pleasant and painful experiences to reveal His will for their character development.

4. *Seek the support you need.* Contact your pastor or a Christian mental health professional to evaluate the possibility of an intervention. Addictions progressively require more and more use of the addictive substance or process to provide similar levels of relief. Over time the addict's health diminishes, family finances become strained, and relationships begin to die. To maintain denial, the addict isolates more and more from those who would tell how they are being hurt. Given enough time, the addict deteriorates and "hits bottom," where denial is finally broken by enough pain. At the bottom, addicts have three choices: die, break mentally, or make the choice to seek God and to enter the recovery process.

Rather than waiting for the natural progression of addiction, the addict's family and friends may be able to intervene. An intervention should only be undertaken with the guidance of an experienced counselor and requires that the whole family agrees to involve themselves in the intervention process.

Find others who have had similar experiences with an addicted spouse. Like Sherri, the addict's spouse assumes that no one has had quite the same experience. Shame keeps us from telling anyone how we are suffering. Fear that others would abandon us if they found out keeps us silent and stuck. Ideally, your church would have a support group to provide the needed emotional and spiritual encouragement.

Confidentially share your situation with your pastor and other spiritual friends. Ask them for their prayer support as you seek wisdom in making nonanxious choices. Prayer is the greatest asset believers have, yet it may be the most underappreciated. The burden of this group may expand to others in similar situations and shape new directions in ministry for the church.

One of every 10 adults in the United States is an alcoholic (2 out of 100 people in Canada). Each alcoholic negatively affects the lives of four to six others. An estimated 30 million Americans are adult children of alcoholics and struggle with the effects of growing up in an alcoholic family. Estimates are that as many as 5.5 million "born again" believers grew up in alcoholic families.[1] Add other addictions and the negative effects of dysfunctional family environments and the population affected is staggering. An unrecognized number of people in the pews of churches each week have been affected by addiction and similar dysfunctional situations. The church can hardly ignore the challenge of presenting the grace of God in ways that address the spiritual formation needs of this population.

In recognition of this challenge the number of churches sponsoring support group ministries has dramatically increased. Support groups do not have the same purpose as Bible studies, prayer groups, sharing groups, or group therapy, although they may experience each of these elements. Bill Morris defines a church-based support group as "a fellowship of people who come together to share our common experience, strength, and hope with one another so that we can identify our struggles, learn about life and relationships, and grow in the ability to trust God and become all that He created us to be."[2]

He identifies the link between a support group and the biblical concept of the Church as a koinonia group in six characteristics: honesty, acceptance, respect, openness, encouragement, and responsibility. Support groups provide vital opportunities to minister to the needs of many who might not otherwise seek help from the Church. They also provide a valuable opportunity for those who found support and hope to minister to others.

Addiction, codependency, dysfunctional issues all call for a response from the Christian community. What a marvelous and unique opportunity to proclaim the grace of God which goes beyond the power of our wrong choices, beyond our weaknesses, beyond our shame to offer us hope and a better way to live in relationship to those around us. In God's power and unfailing love, we can choose to reflect the holiness of character that God calls each of us to live.

*All names have been changed.

Scripture Cited: Psalms 18; 31; 62; 131; 139; Matthew 5—7; Romans 8:26-28; 12:9-21; 15:1-5; Philippians 4:4-9; James 1:2-4

About the Author: Dr. Paul Fitzgerald is a counselor and pastor, who specializes in working with Christian recovery groups.

CHAPTER 8

In Financial Crises

by Richard A. Fish

THE PARABLE of the prodigal son (Luke 15:11-32) illustrates several ways that God may be present in financial crises. At his younger son's request, the father gave him a share of the estate to manage. Our Heavenly Father allows us the freedom to make choices about financial resources. Therefore, some crises result from wrong attitudes about money and unwise lifestyles, while others may come from situations beyond our control. As with the prodigal, we often have to hit "rock bottom" in our handling of finances before we are ready to make changes. Financial crises are very painful to endure, but may provide an opportunity for something better. God knows what we need and is ready to be present with us.

Crises from Wrong Attitudes and Behavior

Many financial crises are brought about, at least in part, by our own unwise behavior. God is often able to enter the crisis when we have gotten ourselves into a desperate situation and need to change our behavior and attitudes. When the prodigal son had experienced the consequences of his financial management and was ready to change, his father joyously welcomed him back.

As a young college professor, I started acting out a long-held idea that someday I would live like a wealthy person. I had grown up with very limited financial resources, but now I thought I had the education and position to live at a much higher level. Unfortunately, it was the 1970s, and I was earning just $9,000 a year. I had the mistaken idea that wealthy people lived in expensive houses in upscale neighborhoods, drove luxury cars, wore expensive clothing, had second homes overlooking the ocean, and of course, had a yacht. They often ate out in expensive restaurants and traveled to Europe regularly. Before long, I was deep in debt, trading more and more of my time and life energy for this lifestyle. My wife had different values, but tolerated my dreams because I dishonestly told her we could afford it. I later discovered in the famous book, *The Millionaire Next Door,* that most wealthy people live quite frugally.

The dream came crashing down one night when the roof of the too expensive house I was trading my life for started to leak in the middle of the bedroom ceiling. God was finally able to enter my financial crisis. I acknowledged that my values and lifestyle were wrong and not in God's will. I promised to change to a simpler lifestyle with a smaller house in a less expensive community and to get rid of all the luxuries. When I had hit bottom in my mishandling of finances, God was able to show me that I was to be a custodian of the wealth and possessions in my life. When I had the proper attitude, God was able to use many of the possessions I had acquired to care for other people.

I had to learn to be aware of my reactions to my financial past. Rather than compensating for past deprivations by spending to live as high as possible, I learned to live as simply as possible. Richard Foster accurately describes this lifestyle as "the freedom of simplicity." When I am buying my used clothing at thrift stores and being thoroughly excited by what I can get cheaply, I often say to myself, "You never get over being poor." Now the mantra is associated with living frugally. When the prodigal "came to his senses" (v. 17) and changed his attitudes and behavior, he was trusted with even more of his father's wealth.

Crises from Economic Conditions

In addition to his wrong behavior, the prodigal's crisis was made worse by "a severe famine in that whole country" (v. 14). Sometimes our crises result from financial conditions beyond our control. Job loss, natural disasters, or uncovered medical expenses may cause crises. These painful times may be opportunities to accept help from others and to consider other alternatives.

Some financial crises give us an opportunity to try something else that might be much better for us. My father would have thought it irresponsible and too frightening to quit a job that was not personally fulfilling, but provided resources to barely support his family. The "opportunity" of a lifetime came after he was fired from his job and then suffered a "nervous breakdown." God entered the financial crisis in the form of my younger brother telling Dad in the hospital, "Don't worry. We'll start a business together, and you'll never have to work for anyone else again."

And so it was. They started their own real estate company. My brother in his early 20s was the president and my middle-aged father was the vice president. With their high level of integrity and sales talent, God blessed the business, and it flourished. My father became a super salesman and a talented accountant. He not only loved his work, but told me after the first year that he paid more in income taxes than he had ever made in total income previously. In the midst of a devastating financial crisis, God had the opportunity to do "a new thing" (Isaiah 43:19) that was far better than what was lost.

A financial crisis may also provide a chance for other people to help us. Many of us find it easier to "give than to receive" (Acts 20:35). When my father was fired from his job and in financial need, a man in the church approached him and gave him $20, saying he cared for him and wanted to help. We knew this man had very limited financial

resources, and we never forgot his kind generosity. Over
the years, God has multiplied thousands of times the giving to others by the sons who were inspired by their father's story of that loving gift.

Crises That Affirm Our Relationship to God

It is important to acknowledge our relationship to
God, even in the midst of great crises. At his lowest point
of financial crisis, the prodigal son "got up and went to his
father" (Luke 15:20). One of my younger brothers had ac-
cumulated millions of dollars in net worth through hard
work and good stewardship. He provided jobs and housing for many people and supported the Lord's work. During a serious recession when real estate values plummeted,
the banks foreclosed on many of his properties. He suddenly found himself in debt for over a million dollars.

He realized that all the assets he had built up with
hard work since he was a teenager were gone. In the
depths of the financial crisis, he reminded the Lord, "I am
only the custodian. If you can find someone else who can
do better than I, give the job to him or her." After several
years of million-dollar tax-loss credits, he is again serving
as custodian of millions of dollars of God's resources.

In the prodigal son parable, the older brother acknowledges the truth that his younger brother's estate dis-
tribution still belonged to the father. He complains about
"this son of yours who has squandered *your* property" (v.
30). The prodigal son went from wealth to poverty and
back to his position as a loved son because of his relationship to his father.

Learning What Is Important

Financial crises may help us appreciate what is really
important in our lives. The prodigal who left his father's

house seeking something more was ready to return and be content to live as a servant (v. 19).

Several years after my financial spiritual awakening, I found myself teaching in a foreign country. I lived in one room with no windows and shared a bathroom with the room next door. I ate simple cafeteria food with the students and had no television or other amenities I was used to at home. For two weeks, my wife was able to be with me. During that time, God showed me that I could be content with a few material comforts, as long as I had family and friends and meaningful work. The apostle Paul expressed this important learning in his letter to the Philippians. "I know what it is to be in need, and I know what it is to have plenty. I have learned the secret of being content in any and every situation, whether well fed or hungry, whether living in plenty or in want" (4:12).

Crises as a Source of Ministry

The Lord can use those times in our lives that we are ashamed of because of our own behavior or the financial crises that were beyond our control as a source for ministry. When I realized that handling finances was an important responsibility in my life as a Christian, I was motivated to study. I took courses to become a Certified Financial Planner and even received a Master's Degree in Financial Planning. Because of my painful personal experiences with financial crises, I am more helpful to others as a financial planner. I can approach people humbly as a "financial sinner saved by grace." I can imagine the prodigal son became a useful resource for other young people as a result of his experiences.

Hurting Rather than Helping

Would the prodigal son have "come to his senses" if the father or some other helpers had "bailed him out" before he hit bottom? Often people endure crisis after crisis because well-meaning helpers enable them to continue their wrongful behavior and attitudes. People seem to need to "hit rock bottom" before there is strong enough motivation to change.

It is very difficult to withhold help from people in financial crisis. When our younger daughter defaulted on a credit card bill, I was tempted to give her a loan. Most of her debt was not even her own. She had permitted a friend to charge on her account. Allowing her to experience the consequences of her financial behavior, however, taught her to be very responsible with finances later in her life. The Holy Spirit needs to guide us in discerning when to provide others with financial help and when to lovingly say no.

Resilience Through Crisis

How we react to a financial crisis often determines if we come through the experience stronger and better. Resilience is not just surviving, but allowing God to use difficult times to make us stronger and better.

Sometimes we find ourselves in a financial crisis seemingly not of our own making. As Rabbi Kushner aptly points out, "Bad things happen to good people." Allow God to be part of a personal survey of what is happening. Are there any ways that our own behavior contributed to this situation? If so, what can we change to make things better? Are there ways that God wants to give other people a blessing by allowing them to help us? Could this be an opportunity to do something else or live differently? Sometimes there is great freedom to try out several new things at such times of crisis. Is this a time to be utterly dependent on God's promise that the "Father knows what you need before you ask him" (Matthew 6:8). Prayerfully trust that He will take care of us even better than sparrows and lilies of the field. Sometimes the help comes mysteriously like "manna . . . from heaven" (John 6:31), but often God provides for us through other people.

Practical Considerations in Financial Crises

Knowledge and choice are keys to dealing with financial matters. Take the time to find out your real financial situation. Add up the value of your assets and subtract the amount of all debts. Next, have each family member write down every penny they spend and every penny of income. At the end of two weeks or a month, put the spending in categories so you can see what is happening and make more informed choices about spending. An elaboration of this approach can be found in the book, *Your Money or Your Life*, by Dominguez and Robin.

Sometimes the financial crisis is so severe it seems hopeless. Because of poor management, the country singer Willie Nelson found himself owing the IRS over $4 million. His response actually provides hope for people in an overwhelming debt crisis. He observed, "If I owed a million dollars, it would be *my* problem. Since I owe 4 million, it's *their* problem." When the amount of debt is so high that there is little or no hope of paying it off in a reasonable amount of time, creditors are obliged to work with you. As in Willie's case, creditors often settle for amounts much lower than what is owed.

In his financial crisis, the prodigal son assessed his situation and did something practical about it. He went to his father, acknowledged his mistakes, and asked to be taken back as a servant. It turned out much better than he expected because of his father's response.

Recommended Reading:

Dominguez, Joe and Vicki Robin, *Your Money or Your Life: Transforming Your Relationship with Money and Achiev-*

ing Financial Independence (New York: Penguin Putnum, Inc., 1992).

Foster, Richard, *The Freedom of Simplicity* (Harper and Row, 1981).

Ramsey, Dave, *Financial Peace: Revisited* (New York: Viking, 2003).

Stanley, Thomas J. and William D. Danko, *The Millionaire Next Door* (Atlanta: Longstreet Press, 1996).

Scriptures Cited: Isaiah 43:19; Matthew 6:8; Luke 15:11-32; John 6:31; Acts 20:35; Philippians 4:12

About the Author: Dr. Fish teaches psychology and sociology at Eastern Nazarene College, Quincy, Massachusetts.

CHAPTER 9

In Serious Illness or Injury

by Mark A. Holmes

IT WAS ONE of those things that I hoped I was wrong about. I was experiencing symptoms that told me my body was not correctly handling the glucose it manufactured. A trip to the doctor and a blood test confirmed my suspicions. I had developed diabetes. For the first time in my life, I had a serious disease. One even potentially fatal, if I fail to comply with its special needs. I am a Christian with a serious, chronic illness. Little did I know, when I accepted the assignment to write this chapter, how relevant the topic would become. Where is God in serious illness or injury?

The question concerns both the nature of God and our perception. Theologically the answer is quite simple—God is in the midst of all our experiences. However, personal perspectives can overlook this, allowing us to experience feelings of abandonment. Sometimes this is because God does not respond to our need the way we want. He is just not where we think He should be. Other times, his absence can be felt because we neglect to seek Him at all. Few people become overtly concerned with God's place within their common cold or stomach virus. These we handle well on our own with bed rest and over-the-counter medications. It is when the chances of recovery decrease, or we contract a disease that is chronic, that we begin to inquire more seriously about God's intervention. The less that can be done by modern medicine, the more interest we have in

God. There is an old saying that there are no atheists in foxholes. Likewise, I have found few atheists in intensive care or oncology units.

This common behavior of humankind implies that God's place in healing begins where human abilities end. If an aspirin or antacid can bring relief, why bother God? We overlook the fact that all healing is an act of God. Medicine is merely a practice that allows humans to join in the endeavor. I remember reading a slogan carved in stone over the chaplaincy department of the Cleveland Clinic in Cleveland, Ohio that stated in essence, humans practice medicine, but God performs the healing. What determines God's place in our illness or injury is not human ability but the malady itself. God is involved within it, just as He is always involved with His people.

The Nature of Illness

Sometimes it is the origin of disease or injury that confuses us on God's participation. We live with the misconception that illness or injury is a foreign experience for humans that must be introduced by an outside influence, either malevolent or divine. If I become ill, either Satan or God had a hand in it. The idea could not be more incorrect. Laying aside the pathological understandings of the nature of disease, the ultimate influence that brings physical problems upon humanity is spiritual, not physical. It results from our interaction with our sinful nature and fallen world.

The cosmos that God created as "good" (Genesis 1) underwent drastic change with the willful rebellion of Adam and Eve (Genesis 3). The nature of humankind was also marred by sin, limiting us in morality and understanding. This fallen world and human nature continues to influence our existence today in several ways.

1. We can become *victims*. The person struck by an intoxicated driver or the cancer patient suffering the results of exposure to chemicals within his or her environment has

little more responsibility for the situation than being in the wrong place at the wrong time. For years, men and women of certain occupations were exposed to asbestos, unaware that breathing its fibers can produce lung cancer. Even our genetic makeup can be influenced by our fallen nature, predisposing us to diseases before we are born. Disease and injury are the inevitable circumstances that result from imperfect people interacting within an imperfect environment.

2. We can become our own worst enemy. Many diseases result from our willful disregard for our well-being. Diets high in fats and cholesterol result in heart disease. Consumption of alcohol can contribute to liver disease and other ailments. Smoking develops higher risks of cancer. Such information is common knowledge, yet millions of people refuse to change their lifestyle to prevent these experiences. Where each of these diseases are biological in nature, their genesis begins with our refusal to treat our body as a temple of God (1 Corinthians 6:19). Our spiritual disobedience can result in our physical undoing.

3. We are not going to get out of this world alive. The result of our sin against God is death (Romans 6:23). The warning God gave to Adam and Eve regarding the Tree of Good and Evil was that the consumption of its fruit would end in their demise (Genesis 3:3). This death sentence is still imposed upon all of humanity. Therefore, we all die. The two means of death are disease or injury. Though we would like to live without experiencing our end, the inevitable day will come when we each will undergo our last malady, and death will overtake us.

Given these three realities of human existence, an awareness of God's place in our experiences can be developed by understanding His involvement in each situation. Where is God in the midst of our limitations due to sin? Is He not involved through enlightenment and direction by way of the Holy Spirit in the life of each individual? Is not the discovery of the harmful influences certain chemicals have on our body an evidence of His involvement with humankind? Or are we so myopic in our understanding that we attribute such findings to mere human ability?

Where is God in our rebellion when we choose to abuse our bodies through neglect? Is God not at work through His grace, calling us to a more appropriate lifestyle? Are the medical abilities not a means of His intervention?

Where is God in death except our resurrection? Does He abandon those who die, or is He the God of both the living and the dead?

The Nature of God

Basic to God's nature are His "omni" attributes. We believe He is omnipotent (all-powerful), omniscient (all-knowing), and omnipresent (ever-present). These attributes are comforting at times, but they also create a challenge. If God is all-powerful, all-knowing, and ever present, then He has the wisdom and ability to prevent any malady from ever happening within creation. However, the fact that they exist informs us that God allows their presence for one of two reasons.

1. Physical suffering is a necessary part of God's will for His creation. This consideration takes us beyond human understanding, making us totally dependent upon God's authority. Those who stress this authority explain God's actions based on His wisdom. In His perfection and knowledge, He knows what is right and perfect and brings it about in His creation. Because we are limited in nature, we do not understand the purpose for each event, so we must respond in faith that God does all things well. After all, He is the Creator; we are merely His creation. His part in our sufferings is understood as a sovereign God working out His perfect will within our lives.

2. On the other hand, there are those who stress human freedom. They recognize God's "omni" attributes, but believe God limits these so that we have a measure of free-

dom by which we run our lives. Our experiences come as a result of our choices or those of others around us. The freedom God allows is a wonderful gift, but it comes with the price tag of responsibility. We are responsible for our choices and experience their results. We can choose appropriate lifestyles, avoiding harmful repercussions, or we can live recklessly and suffer the consequences. God's place in human freedom is best seen as One who intervenes and rescues—if allowed.

Few people reside solely in either one of these two camps. We tend to develop an understanding somewhere in the middle, choosing truths from each extreme, even though they tend to contradict. We like the idea that God is in control of all things, but we also want our options. Thus, we can understand that a disease or injury might come as a result of a choice, but we also want to know why God allowed it to happen. We are torn between assessing blame and seeking deliverance, believing both come from God, but unsure how it is possible.

Accounts from Scripture

Scripture illustrates a number of ways God is found active within human misfortunes in life. Our challenge is whether these accounts teach a general application, or reveal isolated experiences. A case in point is the story of Job. The orchestration of severe suffering in Job's life came as a result of God bragging to Satan about Job's depth of commitment. Challenged by Satan, God allows certain afflictions, first on Job's family and possessions and lastly on Job himself.

A strong argument can be made that this experience is unique, given Job's remarkable relationship with God. However, it also suggests that God can allow misfortunes in our lives as a means of determining our resolve in living for Him. If this is the case, the place of God within our illness or injury could be one of verifier. He is present with the ques-

tion, "Do you still love me in this?" This is not to limit God's
benevolence, as even in the midst of Job's suffering, God
maintained control, setting the limits of Satan's influence.
God may inquire of our love in the midst of suffering, but
always in the environment of His protection and care.

A second illustration of God's use of illness is found in
John 9. Jesus and His disciples encounter a man born
blind. Immediately, the disciples asked what caused the
condition. The disease was presumed to have been the
punishment for sin committed by the man himself (which
would have been difficult since he was born blind) or by
his parents.

The idea of illness or injury being retribution for sin
was common in that day, based on what God had taught Israel regarding His nature: "I the LORD your God, am a jeal-
ous God, punishing the children for the sin of the fathers to
the third and fourth generation of those who hate me, but
showing love to a thousand generations of those who love
me and keep my commandments" (Exodus 20:5-6).

However, Jesus explains that the blind man's condition was not because of sin, but opportunity. "This happened so that the work of God might be displayed in his
life" (John 9:3). The experience teaches us that God can use
circumstances that happen in our lives as means of revelation to the world. Jesus' healing of this man demonstrated
His divine ability and compassionate spirit. God can be
found in our misfortunes, revealing His nature to the
world through our experience.

The apostle Paul introduces a third involvement by
God in illness. Though we do not know what he meant by
his reference to "a thorn in my flesh" (2 Corinthians 12:7),
it was obviously something that limited him. Although he
sought to be healed, Paul eventually accepted his experience as a means of limitation, used by God to protect him
from pride. For Paul, God was found in the midst of his
weakness, enabling Paul to do what he otherwise could

not. Where Paul would be limited, God would take over. The weakness that Paul experienced from his condition would be compensated by God's strength. Instead of lamenting his situation, Paul boasted about it, because God's strength was being made complete within him. The suffering of the disease was worth the limitations in light of the experiences Paul had with God. Humility was the greater blessing.

Probably the most prevalent use of illness within Scripture is the punitive response of God upon people who have sinned. As mentioned above, God expresses this action as basic to His nature (Exodus 20:5-6). Those who rebelled against Him, He punished; those who loved Him, He rewarded. There are numerous examples in Scripture. The death of David's son as a result of David's adulterous affair with Bathsheba (2 Samuel 12:14-23). The plague sent upon Israel as a result of David's census taken against God's will (2 Samuel 24:15). God struck the Philistines with tumors for taking the ark of the covenant (1 Samuel 5:6). He sent venomous snakes among the Israelites because of their discontent (Numbers 21:4-9). Even Paul used blindness as a punishment against the wickedness of Elymas (Acts 13:6-12).

This explanation for illness or injury is not just common in the Scriptures; it seems to be a leading interpretation among people today. Many believe their misfortune is the result of God's judgment for sin. However, God's answer to sin in our present day is not judgment, but forgiveness. God's response to sin is a call to repentance, not a hospital. Jesus absorbed the punishment for sin on the Cross. Although a time of judgment will come at Jesus' return, in this age, God responds with grace.

However, this does not rule out the potential for God to use our situations as means of correction. Hebrews 12:6-11 reveals that God disciplines those He loves. God may use our illness or injury to bring to our attention a correction that is needed in our life. Here God's place is one of counselor and revealer. The position of the one undergoing the experience must be one of surrender and confession. What do our conditions reveal about our lives?

A final divine use of disease and injury is the inevitability of death. As discussed above, death is the ultimate end of all people on this earth (Hebrews 9:27). Psalm 23 reassures us that as we walk through this figurative valley, we do not travel alone. God is with us. John 14:1-6 records Jesus' comforting words to His troubled disciples, promising to go prepare a place for them, so they could live with Jesus forever. In our dying, God becomes our guide and comfort through the transition from this life to the next.

Guardian Angels

Are there provisions by God to protect us from disease or harm, or are we left to our own limitations? Over the history of the Church, there have been those who taught that each person receives at birth an individual angel whose sole purpose is to guard us in life. The scriptural basis for this belief begins in Psalm 91:9-16, which promises the truly committed to God will receive the benefit of protection from harm. God will command His angels to guard us. Satan implies the validity of this claim when he tempted Jesus in the wilderness, challenging Him to reveal His identity by placing himself in a life-threatening situation (Matthew 4:5-7). Jesus' response was that such an action would be an inappropriate test of God.

A second reference is found in Matthew 18:10-11, where Jesus warns us not to discount the importance of children, because *their* angels that exist in heaven always have the audience of God. The warning suggests that children are under the watchful care of God's messengers, who report abuse to the Father himself.

But do these passages mean that followers of God will experience continuous, complete protection? Experience would argue not. People still suffer illness and injury every day. To hold to a complete protection would require one of two explanations for our daily maladies. Either those afflicted are not committed to God to the level the psalm requires, or God's angels are negligent in their duties.

The lack-of-commitment explanation provides a loophole for many faith healers to explain why their ministry failed to restore a desiring seeker. It has also been the source of frustration by those who are apparent victims of their own spiritual limitations. How much commitment does God's guardianship require? How do we measure it? The answer is found in Jesus' lesson on the potency of faith (Matthew 17:19-21). Faith possessed in the smallest portion provides immense power for healing, moving mountains, and more. Faith is the means by which we are saved (Ephesians 2:8); it is also the means by which we continue our relationship with God. His divine protection is provided by our faith in Him, even if only minute in size.

To suggest that God's angels are negligent in their duties is an absurd argument. The mark of God's messengers is total obedience to His will. Not to fulfill what is expected of them is rebellion, an act of sin, which angels cannot commit.

To explain why God's divine and angelic protection is limited we must revisit two topics previously discussed: God's sovereignty and humankind's freedom. In the former case, God's will for what is perfect in this world will always take precedence to our personal desires. Second, as God allows us freedom to choose in life, even the angels are not allowed to go against our choices. The Church has always taught in this regard that the angels can guide, instruct, even argue with our choices, but they can never prevent a decision made. Thus, we do benefit from God's protection in life, though not in an absolute way. God will always allow room for both He and us to express our freedoms.

So, where is God in my diabetes? He is faithfully in the

midst of it, using it for His glory and my spiritual well-being. If I had my choice, I would like Him to heal me. Nevertheless, I also realize that healing can interfere with a deeper experience of God's grace and care. Whatever happens over the remainder of my life, I know that God is in control and working out His will. He is doing the same for you, even in the midst of your serious illnesses and injuries.

Scripture Cited: Genesis 1; 3; Exodus 20:5-6; Numbers 21:4-9; 1 Samuel 5:6; 2 Samuel 12:14-23; 24:15; Psalms 23; 91:9-16; Matthew 4:5-7; 17:19-21; 18:10-11; John 9; 14:1-6; Acts 13:6-12; Romans 6:23; 1 Corinthians 6:19; 2 Corinthians 12:7; Ephesians 2:8; Hebrews 9:27; 12:6-11

About the Author: Rev. Holmes is pastor of The Wesleyan Church in Superior, Wisconsin.

CHAPTER 10

When We Grieve the Death of a Loved One

by Harold Ivan Smith

A MAN FELL INTO A HOLE and could not get out. About the time panic and darkness began to set in, he heard his physician's familiar voice.

"Doc," the man screamed, "it's me! John."

"John, how did you get in this hole?" the doctor demanded, looking down at his patient. "I am going to write you a prescription." The doctor dropped the prescription into the hole and went on his way. Obviously the man had hoped for more. Moments later, he recognized his pastor's voice.

"Pastor! Help me, Pastor, I'm down in this hole."

"John, how did you get in this hole?" the pastor demanded. "I'm going to say a prayer for you." After he prayed a beautiful prayer, he went on his way.

The man was desperate when he recognized a friend's voice.

"Ken, it's me. Get me out of this hole!" Ken peered into the hole, then jumped, landing beside the man. "What did you do that for? Now we're both in this hole!"

"Yes," the friend said, "but I've been here before, and I know the way out."

Early in my work as a grief educator, I learned that the word "why" has more than one syllable along the corridors of a lacerated heart. Grievers have taught me three key convictions:

1. God "permissions" our grief.
2. God accompanies us in our grief.
3. God uses our grief.

However, I must add this stipulation: These things will happen—*if* we cooperate with God in a season called grief.

God Permissions Grief

Death makes shambles of orderly lives, plans, expectations, securities—not just for today or tomorrow, but for the years and decades ahead. Death forces married adults to learn to live alone. Death forces survivors to reinvest themselves, and to ask, "Who am I now that this has happened *to me?* Who am I without (name of loved one)?" A reality is captured in the title of a children's book, *Am I Still a Big Sister?* In grief, many find themselves, in Candice Carpenter's words, "between chapters." "You're not who you were, you're not yet who you are becoming."[1]

Grief makes us feel powerless. Dawn Waltman, following the death of their baby Molly, asked her husband about his struggles. He didn't have to think long before saying, "That I can't fix it. I can't make everything OK for you, for Matthew and Megan, and for me. I just can't."[2] Ironically, in 1963, John F. Kennedy, who as president had forced the Russians to withdraw missiles from Cuba, stood powerlessly and watched Patrick, his two-day-old son, die.

As a child, I frequently heard the song, "Standing somewhere in the shadows you'll find Jesus." As a grief educator, I believe that in the dark hole of grief, God is present. Whenever someone demands, "Where is God when we grieve the death of a loved one?"—even when a series of exclamation marks punctuate the agony of the question—God is there. A popular praise chorus captures the reality, "Emmanuel, God is with us."

Because it deals so deliberately with death and emotions, I read more closely the grief of Mary and Martha following their brother's death (John 11:1-44). The Holy Spirit deliberately moved so that the narrative behind the short-est verse in the Bible, "Jesus wept" (v. 35), could be includ-ed in one of Scripture's longest chapters. Thus, we know Jesus wept when His friend Lazarus died. The clear mes-sage is: if Jesus can grieve, we can grieve!

Grief is a bridge between the past and the future. As we seek answers, all we may be able to see is a thick, emo-tional fog. Yet, in that fog God finds us.

Admittedly, the question, "Where is God in this?" can echo like a summer night's thunderclap. "But God," griev-ers protest, "*this* was not part of the bargain!" Some of the rawest grief I witness is by parents after burying a child, regardless of the age of the child. I recently sat receiving a 93-year-old's lament following the cardiac death of her youngest son. "Why did God take James? Why didn't God take *me*? My life is over. I am of no use to anyone! Why?" I believe God sat with us in that narrative fog.

Unfortunately, some chose never to trust God fully again. One morning, a young boy knelt by his bed and prayed, "Jesus, don't let anything happen to my mother to-day." Hours later after he returned home from school, his father told him, "Peter, Mummy is dead." (She had com-mitted suicide.) Actor Peter Fonda recalled the incident, "It was Friday, April 14. Jesus had failed me. Jesus had let me down. Jesus forgot my prayer about Mother. . . . I never asked Jesus for anything again."[3] I have worked with churchgoers who buried their trust in God with a child, a spouse, a parent.

I find permission in King David's behaviors following the death of his unnamed child. Too often, readers have fo-cused on his adultery rather than the detailed description of his grief as a father. His alarmed servants demanded, "Why are you acting this way?" (2 Samuel 12:21). Al-though David had been warned that the child would die, nevertheless, he pleaded with God, fasted, spent the night lying on the ground, and refused the pleas of servants to get up and eat. His servants feared that he might "do something desperate" (v. 18).

However, if we look at verse 20, we see what David really did. David "got up" from the ground. He could not remain prostrate.

David "washed" and "put on lotions." It is customary in some cultures for the grievers not to bathe or groom. However, many grievers today find a long bath or a shower refreshing.

David "changed his clothes." Clothing has long symbolized change. Jews once tore garments (now they tear a small piece of cloth and pin it to their clothing). Many societies mark significant loss with ritual clothing, especially black.

David "went" to the house of the Lord and "worshiped." This is particularly intriguing because of the clear description that "the LORD struck the child" (v. 15). Jews pray a worshipful prayer called Kaddish for as long as a year after a loved one's death; additionally, they pray Yizor on high holy days. But how do you worship—or continue to worship—a God who "takes" your child?

I cannot forget a young mother who had lost three babies with genetic defects. Going to church became challenging. One Sunday, her sister-in-law turned to her and exclaimed, "Don't you just love praise music?"

"No!" the grieving mother said, slipping to the aisle. "I feel so alienated in my loss around all these 'happy Christians!'"

Ironically, the Kaddish does not mention death but focuses on the greatness of God. Jews believe that if a person will faithfully pray (Orthodox Jews pray Kaddish three times a day and require 10 males to join in the prayer), he or she lives his or her way into a new understanding of God. For Christians, "Great Is Thy Faithfulness" can be a musical kaddish.

Verse 20 goes on to say, David "went to his own

house." Sooner or later the griever has to face familiar environments that have been forever changed. Noted grief theorist William Worden insists that one task facing grievers is to learn to live in environments in which the loved one is absent. Suddenly, a small, cramped bedroom can seem large to a grieving spouse. All the shouts of "Stop using so much water!" to an adolescent during a shower seem meaningless after his or her death.

David made a "request" for food. When people ask the "where is God" question, I point to the food that God's people bring. When people do not know what to say, many cook. Not surprisingly, the food—called "comfort" food—is a way of saying, "I care."

David "ate." After my mother's funeral, I remember one lady at the meal at the church asking, "You need to eat something. Can I fix you a plate?" On many occasions, I had eaten fried chicken and potato salad prepared by those same church ladies, but how good it tasted in my grief!

The inclusion of this extensive description of David's grief demonstrates that God permissions grief. The grief could have been condensed to a simple statement: "David grieved for his son."

God also permissions our grief through music. Although I hear the song less frequently at funerals these days, generations found solace in this musical question, "Does Jesus care when I've said goodbye / To the dearest on earth to me?" Too commonly the song has been labeled "a funeral song" or dismissed as "too sentimental." Yet, the chorus reverberates, "O yes, He cares; I know He cares! His heart is touched with my grief." The composer had learned that Jesus cares not only in initial grief but when grief settles in: "When the days are weary [and] / The long nights dreary."[4] In weary days and dreary nights, God creatively finds ways to disclose His care. Moreover, God deputizes believers to "come alongside" us. No grief experience is alien to God's understanding and concern.

God Companions Grief

The psalmist lamented, "How shall we sing the LORD's song in a strange land?" (Psalm 137:4, KJV). Across the years, Christians have answered that question by singing classics like "Come ye, disconsolate, where're ye languish" as a lamentful hope. With great conviction believers have sung, "Earth has no sorrow that heaven cannot heal."[5] Many grievers cannot explain their theology—or the inconsistencies between their experience and their theologies—but they can, in grief, voice hope for heaven's healing.

The conviction that God is with us in our apprenticeship with grief gives Christians endurance to bear grief. Admittedly, for some, grief breaks an unwritten expectation of God's glitchless favor. No few have grown hoarse from groaning, demanding, screaming, "Why! Why!" No few, listening to such a lament, have shuddered in dismay only to later ask the same question with the same intensity when it came their turn to grieve. God who permissions our grief, permissions the "why-ing" of our grief. After all, Jesus' "why" reverberated across heaven that first Good Friday. God understands the inability of humans to wrap minds and hearts around the pain in particular unexplainable losses. He understands our inability to summon language adequate to phrase our laments. God's heart is touched by our grief.

Author Frederica Mathewes-Green concludes that the useful question is not "why," but rather "What's next?" "What should I do next? What should be my response to this ugly event? How can I bring the best out of it? How can God bring Resurrection out of it?'"[6] Few, sometimes even with postmortem results, get satisfactory answers to their whys. In fact, generations have sung their way into answers, "We will understand it better by and by."[7] While some need to ask their agony-soaked questions, to continue slinging "why" at the heavens prevents the answers to "now what?"

One mother, following her husband's death (in a time period when most women did not work), gave up her "why" questions because she had hungry mouths to feed. Facing her "now what," she chose to turn her home into a boarding house so that roomers would pay the mortgage and keep a roof over her family's heads. One of this mother's children grew up to be famed mystery writer, Mary Higgins Clark. Had her mother obsessed on asking "why" rather than "now what," Mary would have had a far different childhood and adulthood.

We may have to put our "why" questions into escrow for a future conversation. As my colleague Doug Manning insists, "Heaven will have to last a long time. I have so many questions."[8]

God Uses Grief

Grief forces many to reexamine beliefs. Lewis Smedes, a noted theologian, faced a personal Golgotha when his son died "before he had lived the whole of a day." The death of that long-wanted child slammed Smedes into a collision with what he had believed, taught, and counseled —and what as a pastor he had told grievers.

"God's face had had the unmovable serenity of an absolute sovereign absolutely in control of absolutely everything. Every good thing, every bad thing, every triumph, every tragedy, from the fall of every sparrow to the ascent of every rocket, everything was under God's silent, strange and secretive control." An unshakeable certainty in the face of other people's tragedies had worked for Smedes— until he tasted the salt of his own tears and experienced the wracked sorrow of his wife. "God's face has never looked the same to me since." In grief, Smedes concluded, "My portrait of God would have to be repainted."[9] Had Smedes clung to his old ideas or denied his grief, he would have missed countless future opportunities to bring hope to God's grieving children.

On an even greater scale, Adella and Fred Cooper's grief has influenced millions of Americans. Following Adella's sister's death, the Coopers raised her four children. In 1949, the oldest, Robert, learning to drive, misjudged a curve, crashed into a tree and died. The Coopers believed that there had to be a better way adolescents could learn to drive more efficiently. So, using insurance money and donations of cars from local dealerships, the Coopers launched the first driver education program in California, an idea that "caught on" and became a nationwide program. Out of Robert's death came a blessing that continues to bless. Countless lives have been saved through skills and confidence learned in driver education programs. The Coopers told me, "We did what we did where we were with God's help. He helped us go on." God helped the Coopers "de-sting" death's "victory" (see 1 Corinthians 15:54-57).

As an adolescent, Greg Orr accidentally shot his brother in a hunting accident. Years later, Orr entitled his memoirs, *The Blessing*. No few readers were flabbergasted by the title. How can a tragedy that significantly altered a family narrative become a "blessing"? Greg Orr's answer: grief changed him.[10]

In every grief is the potential for God to unfold a disguised blessing. Loss invites grievers, with God's help, to work their way through the strangeness of the experience in order to experience a peace that passes understanding and explanation.

In the French, from which the word "blessing" is derived, the verb *blesser* means "to wound." No one gets through life without a wounding grief; it is merely a question of details and timing. Just as some children and adults bear birthmarks, many will bear "griefmarks."

God uses those griefmarks "so that we can comfort those in any trouble with the comfort we ourselves have received from God" (2 Corinthians 1:3). Many readers cannot imagine how God could "use" their loss, but nothing is lost in the economy of God.

Where is God when we grieve the death of a loved one? Closer than we can imagine.

Scripture Cited: 2 Samuel 12:15-23; Psalm 137:4; John 11:1-44; 1 Corinthians 15:54-57; 2 Corinthians 1:3

About the Author: Dr. Smith is a certified grief counselor, living in Kansas City, Missouri.

CHAPTER 11

When We're Trying to Make Decisions

by Mark R. Littleton

RECENTLY, I HAVE made decisions to . . .

. . . invest some money in stocks and bonds.

. . . give a significant sum of money to my church.

. . . get involved in some book projects that appeared to be good choices.

. . . restrain myself from shouting at my wife when she got "out of sorts."

. . . visit my doctor about my blood pressure (which appeared to be rising).

. . . buy my son a video game.

As I faced each of these decisions—some minor, some major—I usually stopped to think about them and pray. I didn't always get a "go ahead" signal from God, although I sometimes asked for one. Still, the prayer and turning to God were significant. I honestly don't know many Christians who would consider these items for prayer and reasons to seek the will of God. Many would think of such things as trivial, not worth troubling God.

How does God feel about us seeking Him on questions like these? Should we call on God to help us make such decisions?

Look at several verses from the Bible that offer some insight:

- "Call to me and I will answer you and tell you great and unsearchable things you do not know" (Jeremiah 33:3).
- "If any of you lacks wisdom, he should ask God, who gives generously to all without finding fault, and it will be given to him" (James 1:5).
- "Who is wise and understanding among you? Let him show it by his good life, by deeds done in the humility that comes from wisdom" (James 3:13).

I would challenge you to study these verses and let them speak to you about how God feels about us soliciting Him for wisdom, advice, direction on an issue. Where is God when we cry out to Him to help us?

Listen to this verse: "Keep your lives free from the love of money and be content with what you have, because God has said, 'Never will I leave you; never will I forsake you.' So we say with confidence, 'The Lord is my helper; I will not be afraid. What can man do to me?'" (Hebrews 13:5-6).

What does this teach but that God is there, listening and ready to respond? The real question is not where is *God* when we need to make a decision; it's where are *we*? Are we willing to pray? Will we seek Him? Will we cry out to Him for help?

Recently in danger of being late to church, I tried to get my one-and-half-year-old dressed and ready. I found one of her sneakers, but I couldn't find the other one. Muttering under my breath, I prayed, "Please help me find this, Lord. I need it fast. I can't spend half an hour looking."

I peered around at the room, trying to zero in on one of the tiny blue sneakers my little one wore. I couldn't find it. "Please, God, hurry!" I cried, checking my watch.

In my mind, words appeared: *You won't find this now. Go get her other pair and use them.*

My eyes popped a little, not sure whether this was a

deception from Satan, an instruction from God, or an idea in my own head. Immediately, though, I headed to the drawer that contained the shoes, found the second set right away, and hurried back to my daughter. I slipped them on and headed for church, telling myself to remember this little episode for my journal.

Is God concerned about a little girl's shoes? Why not? Why wouldn't He be? These are important things. I wouldn't want to take Elizabeth to church barefoot. I find that I'm often praying about things like this.

The above verses clearly teach:

- God is more than willing to hear our prayers, listen to our concerns, and respond by giving us His wisdom on the subject.
- God has no resentment when we ask Him for wisdom, no matter how big or small the situation. He never says, "Get a life. You're an adult. Think for yourself." No, He's always ready to supply the wisdom we need, like the situation above with my daughter.
- God will never let us hang in the breeze. He will not forsake us or desert us in the crunch. He'll be there for us when we need Him. What kind of father would act like an irritated Scrooge when we come to him for help?

Listen to this important verse: "If you, then, though you are evil, know how to give good gifts to your children, how much more will your Father in heaven give good gifts to those who ask him!" (Matthew 7:11).

Isn't wisdom a gift? Isn't it something we can't always dredge up on our own?

To be sure, God is "an ever-present help in trouble" (Psalm 46:1). It's always right and wise to go to Him with our needs. I think, however, that we also should consider other factors—like timing, the need itself, study, consultation, and patience on our part.

What do I mean?

Timing

Sometimes our timing is not God's timing. We need to wait. Wisdom or direction are not always forthcoming in situations where the problem is not dire.

For instance, the first time I met my wife, Jeanette, she so enamored me that I walked out to my car, climbed in, and cried, "God, I'm going to marry that woman." Now, marriage is a pretty big deal for most of us. I'd already suffered through one bad marriage that ended in divorce, so caution with a big "C" needed to rule in this situation. However, Jeanette so entranced me that I didn't even pray about it (at that point); I just told God what I wanted to do.

However, God's timing needed some consideration. I began praying about Jeanette, getting to know her by sending E-mails back and forth (she lived 1,000 miles away from me), talking on the phone, and weighing the situation. I'd been enthusiastic before about some women I dated that ended up with a "No" answer from God about marriage.

We plodded along. However, after spending two weeks with her on two different trips, I believed I knew what God wanted. The message from heaven seemed to be, "Go ahead. It's a go!" We married seven months after the first meeting.

Where is God when we need to make a decision? He's there, ready and willing to help. Nevertheless, we must also consider God's timing. Many times a decision seems to receive a yawn from heaven until we've worked through some details. God doesn't always answer immediately.

Need

A second factor is need. How dire is your decision-making situation? Do you need an answer right away? I think of the story of Gideon in the Book of Judges, where he needed to know from God about fighting the Midianites. He set out a fleece twice to find out what God wanted.

In the end, a great victory occurred because Gideon sought God. Gideon could not belabor this decision over days or weeks. He needed God's wisdom *immediately*. And God answered quickly. I believe if your need is immediate, God will answer speedily. He does not expect us to hang in there indefinitely when the matter presses upon us.

In my own life, I have bought four different houses over the years. Each time I sought God about this need, expecting and hoping that He'd answer quickly. Happily, God answered each situation with speed and prowess. In fact, with the fourth house, my realtor advised me to make an offer $10,000 less than what the seller asked. She told me, "You'll be lucky if they come down a couple of thousand."

I kept seeking the Lord about it, and I sensed His wisdom guiding me to actually offer $20,000 less than the asking price. My realtor thought I was nuts, saying, "OK, I'll take it to them, but I can't promise anything." To our surprise, the seller took our offer without even negotiating. We got an incredible deal on a fine house, and we thanked God profusely.

How great is your need? Is it urgent? Can you sit on it for a while? Do you need to pray more and think about it? These are all factors, and God may desire more to take you through the process than answer right away. If the need isn't urgent, why shouldn't He let us think, meditate, and ponder our decision over a period of time? On the other hand, if it is urgent, God will not tarry. He promises to answer when we call on Him: "Then you will call upon me and come and pray to me, and I will listen to you. You will seek me and find me when you seek me with all your heart" (Jeremiah 29:12-13).

Study

A third factor is study. Sometimes God's answer won't be an "impression" in our hearts, the "still small voice" talking in our souls, or some other "supernatural" circumstance guiding us in the right way. Sometimes God desires that we do a bit more than pray. He's there the whole time, but He wants us to read our Bibles, consult pertinent verses, and maybe even read some manuals or books about the issue. Matthew 7:7 tells us to ask, seek, and knock. Those are legitimate ways to search God for His wisdom, and they don't mean He always responds to the initial prayer. Sometimes we have to seek and knock.

In the same way, God doesn't always do something supernatural to guide us in some situations. Often, He expects us to use our brains and mine out the wisdom on the issue from other sources.

Recently, I began writing a book about medical personnel in war situations. It's kind of a "Chicken Soup" book for medics and soldiers who were wounded and helped in a battle situation. My partner in the project offered to find the people with the stories, but soon I discovered he wasn't digging up enough. I prayed for God to help me find more people to include. I began looking up stories in books and other places, contacting the local Veteran's Administration hospital and talking to various agencies to find these heroic stories. Soon I found many testimonies that would work in the book.

Often it takes study to find an answer from God for a decision. He won't simply infuse us with the answers, but wants us to use our brains and get out there to discover what's available.

Consultation

Another factor in where God is when we need help making a decision is talking to other believers, leaders, pastors, and friends. God wants us to tap into the wisdom of godly people around us. He may not speak directly to us, but will use such people to meet our need.

Remember the story in Exodus, how Jethro, the father of Moses' wife, Zipporah, gave the Hebrew leader advice as to how to organize the Israelites? He told Moses to appoint leaders over groups of 10, 100, 1,000, and 10,000. He suggested that these shepherds handle the disputes within the groups, and that Moses only deal with the ones no one else could figure out. It was good advice, advice that undoubtedly came through Jethro from God. Often, God uses people outside our immediate frame of reference to give His wisdom to us. How many times have we made a decision on the basis of what our fathers, fathers-in-law, mothers, mothers-in-law, or someone else has offered?

In my family, I recall many times hearing the story of how my father got into sales. He worked for Westinghouse and was being groomed for a managerial position when something came across his desk about another company looking for sales people. My father consulted with both his father and my mother's father. Dad's father was a company man who had long belonged to unions and knew well how companies worked. He'd been through the Depression and knew the value of a solid corporation. He advised my father to stick with Westinghouse. It was a large company, and thus offered tremendous security if the economy went sour in the future.

My mother's father, though, had long been a sales person himself in the laundry industry. He counseled my father to go after the sales position. He said, "Sales drives a company. Without good sales personnel, the company won't make any money, and their security won't stand." He also told my father that because of this, it's the sales staff who end up making the highest salaries through commissions in both large and small corporations.

My father took the sales position and never looked back, finishing his career as president of a company which sold machinery.

Today, I would say the advice that came through my grandfather originated in the mind of God. God often uses others to counsel us, and He supplies us with His counsel through them.

Patience

Ultimately, the No. 1 issue in where God is when we need His direction in making decisions is whether we'll be patient enough to wait on Him and seek His wisdom. Or whether we'll ignore those resources and plunge ahead just because we "feel" it's the right thing.

God teaches us patience through making us live through situations that try our patience. If we didn't need patience, He would never make us wait. However, He often makes us wait specifically so He can develop the patience muscles in our hearts.

One of the best ways God develops patience is through our families, our spouses, our children. We may need to make a decision about a trip, a vacation, an investment, or another need, and it's our family that holds us up. Sometimes when I'm sitting at my computer, typing away on a chapter like this one, my baby Elizabeth will toddle into my office with her arms out, asking me to hold her. She climbs into my lap and sets her head on my shoulder, at peace and looking very comfortable and happy. I want to get on with my project, but I can't type with her in my arms. Sometimes I stew, wishing she'd hurry up and get on her way. At other times, I just grin and bear it.

Today, though, she came in crying with her arms out, so I picked her up and comforted her. I knew I had to get this article done—it was already a week late—but I knew Elizabeth's need had to take priority. That's when God reminded me that He's stitching patience into my psyche and making me a better father and person because of Elizabeth and others in my family.

I don't know about you, but for me, decisions—small, large, insignificant, monumental—are all aspects of walking with God and learning to trust Him. Sometimes in making a decision, He seems to tell me to wait, or study up on it, or pray more, or consult so and so. I rarely find a situation, though, that doesn't get His attention and wisdom. Even if I'm feeling desolate and that He's disappeared from my universe, I still know that He's there. He will lead me, as the psalmist said in Psalm 23: "The LORD is my shepherd, I shall not be in want. He makes me lie down in green pastures, he leads me beside quiet waters, he restores my soul. He guides me in paths of righteousness for his name's sake. Even though I walk through the valley of the shadow of death, I will fear no evil, for you are with me" (vv. 1-4).

Look at those powerful words one more time. They tell us:

- He will not allow us to be in want, that is, in need.
- He leads us to the places where our needs will most speedily be met.
- He guides us to do what's right at all times.
- He is with us, even when a situation is most dangerous.

Those are good words for any Christian about to make a decision of import. They assure us. They empower us. They offer us a rope to hang onto in perilous waters.

I have found that God never leaves me hanging in the wind. Through every decision I've made as a Christian, I've found Him faithful and true, no matter how long it took for the answer to come.

You will too.

Scripture Cited: Psalms 23:1-4; 46:1; Jeremiah 29:12-13; 33:3; Matthew 7:7, 11; Hebrews 13:5-6; James 1:5; 3:13

About the Author: Rev. Littleton is a freelance writer, living in Gladstone, Missouri.

CHAPTER 12

In the Dark Night of the Soul

by Russell Metcalfe

SOONER OR LATER, just about every believer faces some crisis of life that becomes a personal dark night of the soul. What may begin as a normal reaction to loss or change may take on what seem to be spiritual dimensions. Days, weeks, even months may go by with no sense of blessing. When prayer and worship become blocked and meaningless, and when that emptiness continues and continues with seemingly no end in sight, we may be in one of life's supreme tests.

We wonder what has happened. Where is God?

The dark night of the soul is not a fun place to be. We've all had our ups and downs. Mood swings are more or less normal. They come to us all. We feel lousy, but we try to soldier on. We wait for the clouds to pass, and they may tarry, but pass they do.

The dark night of the soul is something else. The lights go out. The screens go black. The lines are dead. God is not answering His phone. And as hard as we look, there is no light at the end of the tunnel. Where is God now? Where can we look for answers? How do we articulate the questions? Are there any points of reference? Where are the lifelines?

Let me begin by distilling all the years of my pastoral perspective into two short statements:

- God is good.
- God loves us.

I really believe that. The dark night of the soul will pass! We may not see the light at the end of the tunnel. But believe me, the dark night of the soul comes to the believer with God's permissive will, and though at the time unseen, with His support of His child in the furnace. We probably won't feel the support. We certainly will be tempted not to believe it, but God knows, and God cares. With God's help, we can hold steady in the darkness.

Sources of Strength

There are no quick fixes or cheap solutions, but there are sources of strength to which we may turn. The fellowship of God's people can be a vital support. As Reuben Welch said by the title of his book a few years back, *We Really Do Need Each Other.* When the usual avenues of prayer seem to have dried up, take the advice of someone who has "been there, done that," and don't add the burden of guilt to the load. There are things we can do to sustain and strengthen us as we wait for the dawn. A trusted counselor may be of great help. Perhaps the resource most likely to reach us will be the written Word.

An old, country pastor was asked for a promise from the Bible to use in tough times. He said, "My favorite verse is, 'It came to pass!'" And pass it will. In addition to his homespun but sage advice, and keeping in mind that there are many promises the Holy Spirit can use for healing, I would recommend two passages from the Scriptures in this attempt to answer the question, "Where is God in the dark night of the soul?"

The first scripture passage with great lifelines is the story of Job. Job's story is the premier handbook on the believer's dark night of the soul. Take hold of the Book of Job as much as possible. It is not a simple book. Crises of faith are never simple. Still, there are some lifelines in Job's story that can be grasped and trusted.

Careful! Not all of the apparently profound statements

in the Book of Job are to be taken at face value. Job's story is given in the form of a drama, and the different characters voice opinions and would-be solutions. Look and listen to how Job faced his profound darkness.

Job resisted simply giving up. He refused to play the blame game. He said, "The LORD gave and the LORD has taken away; may the name of the LORD be praised" (Job 1:21). Even when his wife told him to curse God and die, his reply was, "Don't be foolish!" And later in his agony, he said, "Even if God should kill me, yet I will believe He is good; I trust Him!" (13:13, 15, author's paraphrase).

Job cried out to God in prayer and told Him how he felt. "I don't know where You are! I'd like to present my case in person!" (23:3-4, paraphrase). He prayed, "Show me why I'm going through this!" (10:2, paraphrase). Yet even when Job couldn't find God anywhere, he determined to hold his faith. "God knows where I am," was his testimony. "When this test is over, I will come forth as gold" (23:10, paraphrase).

Some of the most sublime words in all Scripture are Job's testimony in his darkest hour, "I know that my redeemer liveth, and that he shall stand at the latter day upon the earth: And though after my skin worms destroy this body, yet in my flesh shall I see God: whom . . . mine eyes shall behold, and not another" (19:25-27, KJV).

At the end of the drama, none of the characters, including Job, had it all figured out. The "why" of it all was a mystery to the humans involved, and remained a mystery. Job and his counselors thought they needed answers. They tried to analyze and diagnose and prescribe. Yet at the end of the story when God breaks in and speaks, Job is satisfied! God never explained, and Job didn't ask. What Job needed, and what we need in soul darkness, is for God to move in with that unmistakable, powerful presence. Just to *know* God knows and cares, and that He is with us brings an end to both the question and to the dark night itself.

God's Displeasure?

Job's story makes it plain that the dark night of the soul is *not* an indication of God's displeasure. God permits these times, but God does not bring them about as punishment. There is absolutely no indication that Job's trial came because he had broken God's laws. Quite the contrary. Satan was permitted to use terrible circumstances to attack Job's relationship with God. He was unsuccessful.

Circumstances may trigger spiritual darkness in believers' lives. Severe illness, loss, a heart attack may bring us to feel God's absence. Circumstances come to all. They do not prove anything bad or good about our walk with God. If we have sinned, God is faithful to show us exactly where, and is faithful and just to forgive us as we confess. The dark night of the soul is not so easily understood.

Job's story is a window on the place of friends and counselors in the times of darkness. Job's "comforters" were a sorry lot. As long as they just kept him company and kept quiet, they were probably some help. But then came the great words of "profound wisdom," usually ending with a diagnosis of guilt! And sure enough, it will be very easy to find some modern relatives of Job's comforters who will very kindly give advice. Often that advice is some form of "you get what you deserve" or in other words, "It's your fault! Snap out of it!" Yet remember, the dark night of the soul is not an indication of God's displeasure, nor of judgment for sin.

One important but mysterious lesson from Job is this: we don't know how our holding steady may bring honor to God. In the scriptural account, Job never knew about how proud God was of him, how God valued Job's relationship with himself. Job never knew that he was proving to heavenly beings the question that Satan asked: "Does Your servant Job serve You because he loves You, or just for what he gets out of it?" (Job 1:9, paraphrase).

In the Book of Ephesians, Paul hints that maybe this sort of cosmic testimony is still going on: "Through the church, the manifold wisdom of God should be made known to the rulers and authorities in the heavenly realms" (3:10). A careful reading of this passage would seem to indicate that whenever God's people are faithful in trial, God's wisdom is being manifested in realms beyond our human understanding. When you and I, as members of the Body of Christ, hold steady in our dark nights of the soul and prove that God is good and faithful, then Job's faithful testimony is presented again and again. In the dark night of the soul, God is watching with love. And Jesus is at the right hand of the throne of God, where He is praying for us.

A second scripture passage is Hebrews 12:1-3, and the passion, ascension, and session of Jesus that it invokes. Remember who and what Jesus said He is: the Good Shepherd, the Way, the Truth, the Life, the Light of the World. Listen again to His invitation: "Come to me, all you who are weary and burdened, and I will give you rest" (Matthew 11:28). However above and beyond even that, in a dark night of the soul, take hold of the passion and session of Jesus. The Passion is what Jesus did for us. He "endured the Cross," and despised the shame so that He can be "the author and perfecter of our faith" (Hebrews 12:2). Then Jesus ascended to the Father, where He is in Session. The Session is what Jesus is doing now for us: making intercession, praying for each of us (Romans 8:34). The Passion and Session of Jesus are a strong lifeline.

Hebrews 12:1-4 has proved a powerful, practical help to me. In this passage, we are reminded that (1) Jesus is "the author and finisher of our faith" (v. 2, KJV). What He has begun He is capable of completing. (2) Jesus knows the darkness. He endured the dark night of the soul himself. In the Garden of Gethsemane, Jesus prayed alone. On the Cross, He cried, "My God, why . . . ?" (Matthew 27:46;

Mark 15:34). (3) Jesus triumphed, not only for himself, but for us. He is in Session! He is now seated at the right hand of the throne of God, where He is making intercession for those of us who by faith are following after Him.

"Consider him . . . so that you will not grow weary and lose heart" (v. 3). The writer of Hebrews urges us in the dark night of our own souls' agony to look to Jesus, and trust that He knows and cares what we are going through. And to hold steady, regardless of how strong the winds are blowing and how pitch-black the night.

Let's Be Practical

In looking to the Scriptures, to the example of Job, and above all, to Jesus himself for guidance in our darkness, there are some very practical measures we can determine to take.

We can determine to hold steady—no matter how we feel. The dark night of the soul is a poor place to think about quitting. No one gets off the train when it is halfway through the tunnel. Take courage, and as much as possible defy the darkness; affirm praise of God—even in that darkness.

In addition to the purely spiritual dimensions of finding an answer to the question where God is in the dark night of the soul, let an old pastor offer some personal, practical advice:

Do get physically tired. A wise medical doctor once told me, "It is almost impossible to have tired thigh muscles and maintain a high level of anxiety." I know the dark night of the soul is not exactly the same as mental and emotional depression, but emotional depression almost always is part of the package and needs to be addressed. Mental exhaustion is real exhaustion, but getting the muscles tired to match the mental and emotional stress can bring about a more healthy sort of tiredness that enables the "sleep that knits up the raveled sleeve of care" (Wil-

liam Shakespeare, *Macbeth,* Act 2, Scene II). *Don't* overex-
tend or tire yourself, schedule-wise. Leave extra time for a
nap *after* a long walk, jog, or reasonable exercise.

When the rugged prophet Elijah lay under a juniper
tree, physically exhausted and emotionally drained, feeling
spiritually isolated, he certainly experienced a dark night
of the soul. God's prescription was sleep. He was already
physically tired. When he woke, an angel had prepared a
light lunch, and then, more sleep. Then, Elijah was ready to
wait for the still, small voice.

Do find a compatible prayer group to join. Your pastor
may be the one to guide you into a small-group support
setting. *Don't* isolate or shut yourself away from friends
and family. By the same token, be very selective in sharing
your heart. You don't need Job's comforters. A good Christian counselor can sometimes help point to that light at the
end of the tunnel.

Do tell God how you feel. He can handle your feelings, but remember He is on your side, whether you believe it at the time or not. Remember, He will have the last
word! *Don't* worry if and when your prayers are difficult
or impossible. One thing is certain; we've said it before: the
dark night of the soul will not last forever.

Conclusion

Let me close with a final thought that is so simple it
just might prove a help. Remember that between Psalm 22
and Psalm 24 is Psalm 23. Now, isn't that profound? However, Psalm 22 is the dark night of the soul. It begins with
the words of David that became the cry from the Cross:
"My God, My God, why have you forsaken me?" Psalm
24, just one short chapter away, begins with a magnificent
shout of assurance: "The earth is the LORD's, and everything in it." David is saying, "All's right with the world!
Living is great!" It seems a long way from Psalm 22 to
Psalm 24, emotionally and in terms of assurance. Maybe it

is just a coincidence, but isn't it interesting that in between Psalm 22 and Psalm 24 there it is—Psalm 23? The way from darkness of soul to full assurance is in the personal presence of the Shepherd of the soul. Sixteen times in those six short verses that we all know by heart, David uses the personal pronoun to affirm, "The Lord is *my* shepherd" (v. 1, emphasis added) and "He restores *my* soul" (v. 3, emphasis added). The way these scriptures are arranged is a reminder that the path from desolation to assurance is in the personal, assuring presence of the Shepherd.

"The Lord is *my* shepherd" begins the journey from darkness to glory.

Scriptures Cited: Job 1:9; 1:21; 10:2; 13:13, 15; 19:25-27; 23:3-4, 10; Psalms 22:1; 23:1, 3; 24:1; Matthew 11:28; 27:46; Mark 15:34; Romans 8:34; Ephesians 3:10; Hebrews 12:1-3

About the Author: Rev. Metcalfe is a retired Nazarene pastor, living near Boston, Massachusetts.

CHAPTER 13

When Everything Is Going Well

by Rhonda Wheeler Stock

WALK DOWN THE AISLES of any Christian bookstore, and we will find volume after volume that tells us how to cope with crisis. We can find books that tell us where God is when we hurt, where God is when we're broke, where God is when we're in an abusive relationship. The magazine racks are filled with periodicals featuring articles with advice for when we're overwhelmed, underappreciated, or just plain mad. Everyone, it seems, knows how to reach God in times of trouble, and everyone is happy to guide us in the right direction.

However, what about when life is pretty good, even great? What about those rare but wonderful times in our lives when we are experiencing the best God has to give? Our kids are emotionally and physically healthy, our relationships are positive, our jobs are secure, and our spiritual lives are dynamic and enriching. Life couldn't get much better.

How do we cope with *that?*

"But wait!" you say. "What's there to cope with? Isn't that the way it's *supposed* to be? Aren't we as Christians *supposed* to enjoy the blessings of God? If everything's great, what's the problem?

Maybe there isn't a problem. Or maybe "problem" isn't the right word. Maybe the word should be "challenge," as in "What *challenge* do we face when everything is going well?"

Crisis propels us into His arms. When things go wrong, we cry out to Him and cling to His promises. We agonize before Him in prayer. We search His Word for answers and for assurance that He is still in control. Then the crisis passes. We are no longer driven to prayer or Bible reading. We are grateful He was there for us when we most needed Him, but now things are back to normal. The desperation is gone. The awful, overwhelming need is gone. Our prayers become perfunctory. Our Scripture reading is limited to quick glances at a trendy devotional book. God is once again relegated to the periphery of our lives.

Take, for instance, Dan and Roxanne who were newlyweds and fresh out of college, Dan found a terrific job five hours from the hometown where the two of them had grown up. Faced with a new life in a new city, they had to stay in a motel while searching desperately for an apartment they could afford. All their worldly goods were stashed in a small rental trailer in the motel parking lot. It would be two weeks before Dan drew his first paycheck. In the meantime, they had to eat, pay for the motel and trailer, and reserve enough from their meager savings for a deposit on an apartment when they found one. When they were down to a package of baloney and a bottle of ketchup, they knew they had reached the limit of their resources.

"Relying on God was the only thing we could do," Roxanne says now. From the moment they hitched the trailer to their rusted-out, old, small car, they were in prayer that God would provide for them. "It was humbling," admits Roxanne. "We couldn't even afford a cup of coffee. The last semester of college nearly drained the last of our savings, and we were getting desperate."

Eventually, of course, Dan and Roxanne found an affordable place to live, the paychecks started coming, and they had more in the refrigerator than baloney and ketchup. "It would have been easy to cruise along spiritually once things started going our way," says Roxanne.

"When you don't feel that sense of desperation, it's easy for your spiritual life to become sort of ho-hum."

The challenge, then, is staying hungry for God even when life is as smooth as vanilla ice cream. God doesn't step away from us when the crisis is over. It is not His design that He hover in the background, quietly waiting for the next disaster to hit us. He longs to be an integral part of our lives, whatever our circumstances. He wants us to crave a relationship with Him all the time, not just when things get rough and we need His intervention. The challenge is keeping ourselves in a place where He is ever before us. Even when life is good, we must rely solely on Him as our source and our strength. To do this, we must recognize three principles:

1. God never changes.
2. Good things come from God.
3. Good times don't last.

God Never Changes

Scripture reveals this truth throughout its pages. In Exodus 3:14-15, God tells Moses, "I AM WHO I AM and WHAT I AM, and I WILL BE WHAT I WILL BE . . . Say this to the Israelites, I AM has sent me to you! . . . The Lord, the God of your fathers, of Abraham, of Isaac, and of Jacob, has sent me to you! . . . By this name I am to be remembered to all generations" (AMP). Malachi 3:6 says, "I the LORD do not change." Ecclesiastes 3:14, "I know that everything God does will endure forever; nothing can be added to it and nothing taken from it. God does it so that men will revere him." Isaiah 40:28, "Do you not know? Have you not heard? The LORD is the everlasting God, the Creator of the ends of the earth. He will not grow tired or weary, and his understanding no one can fathom." Hebrews 13:8 reminds us, "Jesus Christ is the same yesterday and today and forever." James 1:17 says, "Every good and perfect gift is from above, coming down from the Father of the heavenly lights, who does not change like shifting shadows."

There is an old story of the New Englander who told his wife on his wedding day how much he loved her. As the years went by, the man never again said those three important words. Finally, on their golden wedding anniversary, the wife said, "Husband, on our wedding day you told me you loved me, but you've never once repeated those words to me in our 50 years together."

"Well," said the husband, "if I change my mind, I'll let you know."

God hasn't changed His mind about us. Over and over in the Bible He tells us how much He loves us, how He will be our Provider and our Comforter. The final words of the Bible were set in place some 2,000 years ago. In all those centuries, He has never indicated that anything has changed.

God never changes. We may change. Our circumstances may change. We may veer from the path of righteousness, stumble and lose our way, but God never changes. His love is everlasting; His provision is constant. When we wonder where God is, it's because we have shifted to a place where we cannot see Him. We moved; God didn't.

Good Things Come from God

When life is sailing along on an even keel, we are tempted to give ourselves the credit. We're successful because we attended the right college, or we chose the right network of friends. Our kids are successful because we enrolled them in the right schools and gave them the right combination of affection and discipline—and let's not forget about that terrific set of genes they inherited from us! And if we do give God any credit at all, it's with the attitude, "He owes me because I try to live such a good life."

Do we stop to think that maybe our boat is sailing

along so smoothly because the wind is gentle and the sea is calm? That maybe the good things in our lives are not because of our own efforts but because the God of creation has given us a period of comfort and prosperity?

Mark and Huldah Buntain were evangelical missionaries to Calcutta, India, until Mark's death in the 1990s. Together, they established a ministry that provided food and shelter to some of the world's neediest people. They worked with Mother Teresa to provide top-of-the-line medical services in this needy corner of the world. And, of course, they shared the love of Christ to millions of Indian nationals.

In the 1980s, Huldah was visiting her daughters in America when she shared the story of how one day she longed for some cottage cheese, a delicacy not found in the sweltering venues of Calcutta. She couldn't shake her craving for the cold, creamy stuff. Not long after that, she opened a "care package" from America and found someone had included a container of dehydrated cottage cheese! Huldah was thrilled with the gift, and praised her God for granting her this simple desire. Huldah knew that the source of even the smallest blessing is God himself.

When the apostle James tells us that "Every good and perfect gift is from above," he is using a phrase that can mean "from the beginning" or "from the top down." Either definition is apt when we are discussing the blessings of God. From before the beginning of time, every blessing in the universe has come from God's hands. Even those who have not accepted Christ—or, to use the old-fashioned word, the sinners among us—enjoy God's blessings. Anyone who prospers does so because God allows it, whether it is financial prosperity or prosperity in other ways. Good things come from God.

When everything is going well in our lives, we should remember that we can achieve nothing in our own efforts.

Deuteronomy 8:18 says, "Remember the LORD your God, for it is he who gives you the ability to produce wealth, and so confirms his covenant, which he swore to your fore-fathers, as it is today." No matter how much we plan or how hard we work, prosperity is in the hands of God. When everything is going well in our lives, it is because God has allowed it to be so, not because of our efforts.

Good Times Don't Last

If it is true that every good thing comes from God, is it then true that every bad thing comes from God's enemy? As Paul would say (in the King James Version), "God forbid!" (See Romans 6:2ff.) Good things come from God, yes, but that doesn't mean that God *only* allows good things to come our way. Sometimes God allows negative circumstances into our lives. He does not necessarily *cause* the negative events, but He chooses, for His own reasons, to *allow* the negative circumstances.

Dan and Roxanne, the newlyweds from the beginning of the chapter, both wanted a large family. In quick succession, Roxanne gave birth to two boys. When Roxanne discovered she was pregnant again, the whole family was delighted. This pregnancy brought a special joy to Dan and Roxanne because, for the first time in their young married lives, they weren't struggling financially. They had recently purchased their first home, their two boys were happy and healthy, and the pregnancy was progressing beautifully.

Just into her second trimester, Roxanne was standing at the stove, fixing supper, when she felt her water break. What was happening? Her last visit to the doctor had shown everything was fine. She was healthy, the baby was healthy, everything was as it should be. Panicked, she ran to the bathroom and called for Dan. Within minutes, Dan was holding the tiny body of his stillborn son. They called someone to sit with the boys and rushed to the hospital. The doctor kept Roxanne overnight for observation, but no one could offer any explanations. "Sometimes it happens," the doctor said sadly.

The good news was that Roxanne was fine and would be able to have more children. Today, Dan and Roxanne have four children, all of them healthy. Nevertheless, both Dan and Roxanne still grieve for the little boy that died before he ever really lived. "It's not a devastating grief," says Roxanne matter-of-factly, "but it's there. A small ache in our hearts when the holidays roll around. We just know that he's waiting for us in heaven, and we'll see him someday."

Do Dan and Roxanne blame God for their baby's death? "Absolutely not!" says Roxanne. "Doesn't it say in the Bible that it rains on the just *and* the unjust? Sometimes tragedy happens to God's people. I wish it didn't, but it does. That's life. Deal with it."

Could God have saved their baby's life? Without question, yes. God could have intervened, but He didn't. For whatever reason, He chose to allow Dan and Roxanne to go through this tragedy. The *whys* and *wherefores* will have to wait until eternity to be answered.

Jesus Understands All of This

In John 11, we read the story of Lazarus's death. Lazarus and his sisters were very dear to Jesus; the Savior enjoyed their hospitality whenever He visited Bethany. When Jesus received word that Lazarus was dying, others probably expected Him to drop everything and rush to His friend's side. But He didn't. He waited. And waited. For two long days, He waited. At last, He and His disciples set out for Bethany.

Jesus already knew that His dear friend was dead, but He also knew that God had allowed this tragedy for a specific purpose. Jesus told His followers, "For your sake I am glad I was not there, so that you may believe" (v. 15). When Jesus finally arrived, He was greeted with Mary's hysterical accusations and Martha's stoic acceptance of her brother's death. The mob of mourners sniffed that He could have done something if He had arrived in time.

Jesus was not unmoved by the accusations and sorrow. John 11:35, the shortest verse in the Bible, tells us that "Jesus wept." Jesus knew He was about to perform one of His greatest miracles. He knew that within moments, Mary and Martha's grief would turn to unmitigated joy. Yet for those few moments, Jesus grieved for the loss of His friend, grieved for the sorrow of these people. He knew that God had something great in store for these friends, but still He was saddened by their heartache.

God allowed Lazarus to die even though He could have prevented it. God could have sent Jesus to Lazarus's bedside to deliver a healing touch. For that matter, God could have kept Lazarus from getting sick in the first place, but God chose not to do that. For whatever reason, God chose to allow Lazarus to get sick and die.

In the same way, God sometimes allows sorrow to enter our lives. Sometimes, tragedy is a test of our faith. Sometimes, it's an opportunity for us to draw closer to Him. And sometimes God chooses not to reveal His purpose to us. In those times, it is our responsibility to trust that He has our best interests at heart, that He truly will do what is best for us.

If God is in control of our lives when tragedy strikes, He is even more in control when life is good. Our lives are ordered by God. The good, the bad, the ordinary—all of it occurs as *He* wills it.

If nothing happens to us unless God allows it, then our goal should be to make Him the center of our lives no matter what our circumstances. Crisis should not be the only thing to make us hungrier for God. Good times should not cause us to relax in our Christian walk and neglect the things of God. We should seek God in whatever circumstances we find ourselves, in good times and in bad, in tragedy and in triumph.

Scripture Cited: Exodus 3:14-15; Deuteronomy 8:18; Ecclesiastes 3:14; Isaiah 40:28; Malachi 3:6; John 11:1-44; Romans 6:2; Hebrews 13:8; James 1:17

About the Author: Rhonda Stock is a freelance writer, living in Lenexa, Kansas.

Endnotes

Chapter 1

1. Ron Sider, *Christ and Violence* (Scottdale, Penn.: Herald Press, 1979), 47.

2. Jon D. Hull, "A Boy and His Gun," *TIME* (August 2, 1993), 21-27.

3. "Believers Strive to Stem Violence," *The Christian Century* (January 26, 1994), 69.

4. Ruth Bonapace, "Churches as the 'Only Hope' for Change," *The New York Times* (February 6, 1994), 3.

Chapter 2

1. Friedrich Nietzsche was a German philosopher of the late 19th century who did not believe in and challenged the foundations of Christianity and traditional morality.

2. See Konrad Lorenz, *On Aggression,* Marjorie Kerr Wilson trans. (New York: Harcourt Brace, 1963).

3. James Dobson, "Why I Use 'Fighting Words,'" *Christianity Today* (Des Moines: Vol. 39, No. 7, June 19, 1995), 27.

4. John Wesley, *Works,* vol. IX (Kansas City: Beacon Hill Press of Kansas City, 1986), 222.

5. Wesley, 220.

6. Interview with Robert Schuller Jr., Crystal Cathedral, January 25, 2004.

Chapter 5

1. Jeanette Gardner Littleton, *When Your Teen Goes Astray* (Kansas City: Beacon Hill Press of Kansas City, 2004), 72-80.

2. Laura Schlessinger, *The Proper Care and Feeding of Husbands* (New York: Harper Collins, 2004), 68.

3. James Dobson, *When God Doesn't Make Sense* (Wheaton, Ill.: Tyndale House, 1993), 235.

4. Josh McDowell and Bob Hostetler, *Handbook on Counseling Youth* (Dallas: Word, 1996), 362-63.

Chapter 6

1. B. A. Robinson, "U. S. Divorce Rates: For various faith groups, age groups, and geographic areas" <http://www.religioustolerance.org/chr_dira.htm>, March 20, 2002.

2. James C. Dobson, "The Family in Crisis," <http://family.org/fofmag/pp/a0023971.cfm>, 2001.

3. Alex R. G. Deasley, *Marriage and Divorce in the Bible and the Church* (Kansas City: Beacon Hill Press of Kansas City, 2000), 21.

4. Deasley, 14, 20.

5. Deasley, 25.

6. Deasley, 55.

7. Deasley, 14, 20.

8. Dobson, "The Family in Crisis."

9. Dobson, "The Family in Crisis."

10. Dennis Rainey and Bob Lapine, "The Cost of Divorce on Children," FamilyLife Today transcript, original broadcast date 01/11/02, <http://www.familylife.com/fltoday/default.asp?id=5466>.

Chapter 7

1. Sandra D. Wilson, *Counseling Adult Children of Alcoholics,* ed. Gary R. Collins, Resources for Christian Counseling, vol. 21 (Dallas: Word, 1989), xii.

2. Bill Morris, *The Complete Handbook for Recovery Ministry in the Church* (Nashville: Thomas Nelson, 1993).

Chapter 10

1. Candice Carpenter, *Chapters: Create a Life of Exhilaration and Accomplishment in the Face of Change* (New York: McGraw-Hill, 2002), 39.

2. Dawn Siegrist Waltman, *In a Heartbeat: A Journey of Hope and Healing for Those Who Have Lost a Baby* (Colorado Springs: Faithful Woman/Cook Communications, 2002), 43.

3. Peter Fonda, *Don't Tell Dad* (New York: Hyperion, 1998), 45.

4. Frank E. Graeff, "Does Jesus Care?" 1901.

5. Thomas Moore, "Come Ye, Disconsolate," 1816.

6. Frederica Mathewes-Green, *At the Corner of East and Now* (New York: Jeremy T. Tarcher, 1999), 57.

7. Charles Tindley, "We Will Understand It Better By and By," 1905.

8. Doug Manning, *Don't Take My Grief Away* (San Francisco: Harper and Row, 1979), 47.

9. Lewis B. Smedes, *My God and I: A Spiritual Memoir* (Grand Rapids: Eerdman, 2003), 38.

10. Greg Orr, *The Blessing: The Memoir* (San Francisco: Council Oak Books, 2002).